Copyright © 2024 by Marissa Rose Media

All rights reserved.

No portion of this book may be reproduced in any form without written permission from the publisher or author, except as permitted by U.S. copyright law.

Table of Contents

Introduction   VI
    The New Frontier of Sales

Part I
The Foundations of Online Sales

    1. Understanding Your Market   2
    2. Building Your Irresistible Online Presence   8
    3. Crafting Your Value Proposition   15

Part II
Mastering Content Creation & Engagement

    4. Content is King   22
    5. Social Media Marketing Techniques   29
    6. Email Marketing – The Silent Closer   37

Part III
The Art & Science of Selling

    7. The Psychology of Selling   46
    8. Mastering the Close: In Videos   54
    9. Mastering the Close: In Person, Lives & Over the Phone   61

Part IV
Scaling & Optimization

    10. Turning Leads into Loyal Customers   68

    11. Automation and Technology   75

    12. Analyzing & Improving Strategies   82

Part V
Real-World Applications & Case Studies

    13. Success Stories   91

    14. Common Mistakes and How to Avoid Them   100

    15. Creating Your Personalized Sales Blueprint   107

Part VI
Conclusion & Bonus Chapters

    16. Conclusion   116

    17. Ready to Dive Deeper?   121

    18. Bonus Chapter Part 1   126

    19. Bonus Chapter Part 2   133

    20. Glossary of Terms   140

The best marketing doesn't feel like marketing.
- Tom Fishburne

Introduction

The New Frontier of Sales

Welcome, digital rockstar, to the exhilarating world of online sales! Whether you're juggling meal prep with market research or squeezing in social media strategies between school drop-offs, you've landed in the right place. Today, more than ever, the digital landscape serves as a goldmine for those savvy enough to dig deep and uncover its treasures. And let me tell you, there is no better time to be in the business of selling online.

As a stay-at-home mom of four fabulous tornadoes, I've mastered the art of multitasking. Trust me; if you can negotiate a peaceful bedtime with toddlers, you can close a million-dollar deal in your sleep. However, the transition from traditional to digital selling has radically transformed the game. Platforms like Instagram and LinkedIn aren't just for highlight reels and professional bragging—they're arenas where the champions of commerce are made.

You're here because you're ready to seize the opportunities that the digital world offers. You want to harness the power of social media and email marketing to turn clicks into customers and followers into fanatics. Your ambition is your strongest asset, and boy, are we going to skyrocket it to new heights!

Why This Book?

You picked up this book because you're eager to unlock the secrets of online sales—to tap into strategies that will help you close deals, earn big, and grow your business while maybe even still rocking that messy bun. Entrepreneur, small business owner, sales professional—no matter your starting point, "Digital Dealmakers" is your road map to success.

This book isn't about high-minded theory or academic fluff. Nope. This is your hands-on playbook, full of actionable techniques and real-world tactics that have been battle-tested and proven to deliver results. Think of me as your hype-woman for hustling, right there with you as we navigate the twists and turns of the online sales world.

What You'll Learn

Our journey together spans multiple chapters, each loaded with the kind of easy-to-implement strategies that will transform your online presence and sales approach.

***

Here's a sneak peek into what awaits you:

- **Understanding Your Market**: Align your efforts with your audience's needs and desires. Get inside their heads and hit them right in their sweet spot.
- **Building Your Online Presence**: Create magnetic social media profiles and a personal brand that is as compelling as it is consistent—people will not just follow you, they'll fan-girl (or fan-boy) over you.
- **Crafting Magnetic Content**: Learn how to create content that doesn't just engage but commands action. Because let's face it, likes are nice, but sales pay the bills.
- **Email Marketing Mastery**: Unlock the latent power of your email list to nurture leads and convert them into die-hard, loyal customers.
- **The Psychology of Selling**: Dive into the emotional and psychological triggers that drive people to click "buy." Use them to your advantage like a mentalist at a magic show.
- **Closing Techniques that Work**: Master closing techniques that work effortlessly, even in the hyper-fast world of digital communication.
- **Scaling and Automation**: Discover how to automate your processes, leaving you more time to pour out that last scoop of formula or savor a much-deserved glass of wine.
- **Real-World Applications and Case Studies**: See real-life examples of people who were in your shoes and kicked those shoes off, choosing stilettos instead, on their way to the top.

***

Let's Get Started

Before we dive headfirst into this journey, let's take a moment to picture the future you—a digital dealmaker extraordinaire. You're no longer just managing the chaos but orchestrating it like a maestro. Your inbox is a **treasure trove** of sales leads and congratulatory emails. Picture yourself confidently closing deals, fostering relationships, and watching your business flourish beyond your wildest dreams.

That future isn't a fairy tale. It's real, and it starts here, right now. So put down that laundry basket, grab a cup of coffee (or a glass of wine—I won't judge), and settle into your favorite chair. We're about to embark on an *exhilarating* adventure that will transform the way you think about sales, marketing, and perhaps even yourself.

Welcome to Digital Dealmakers.

Let's get going and make some serious digital waves. Together, we'll transform your business—and your life—starting ***right now***.

Part I

THE FOUNDATIONS OF ONLINE SALES

1

Understanding Your Market

Why Knowing Your Audience is Your Secret Weapon

Ready to pull back the curtains and reveal the **magic** behind successful online sales? Spoiler alert: it's not just in the pitch, the product, or the platform. It's in knowing who you're selling to like the back of your hand. Think of it this way—would you try to sell an ice cream maker to an Eskimo? Of course not. Understanding your market is the secret sauce that turns your sales strategy from a shot in the dark into a *targeted* hit list.

First things first: you need to know exactly who your audience is, where they hang out online, what makes them tick, and what keeps them up at night. Get this right, and everything else will fall into place like perfect puzzle pieces.

Demographics and Psychographics: The Dynamic Duo

Start with the basics—demographics. These are the quantifiable characteristics of your audience. Age, gender, income, education level, occupation, marital status, and location are key factors. Knowing these can steer your marketing strategy in the right direction.

But don't stop there. Psychographics are where the real gold is. These dig deeper, exploring your audience's lifestyle, values, interests, and behavioral traits. Are they fitness enthusiasts? Do they value sustainability? Are they driven by social status or driven by bargain hunting? Understanding these nuances allows you to connect on a more emotional and personal level, giving you the edge over your competition.

Creating Killer Customer Personas

Now that we've gathered all this juicy intel, it's time to create customer personas—your fictional but data-driven representations of your ideal customers. Think of them as characters in your sales story. Give them names, backgrounds, hobbies, and even favorite social media platforms.

Let's say you're selling an online course for aspiring digital nomads. One of your personas could be:

- **Name**: Sarah, the Wanderlust Entrepreneur
- **Age**: 32
- **Occupation**: Freelance graphic designer

- **Income**: $70,000 per year

- **Location**: Los Angeles, but dreams of working from a beach in Bali

- **Interests**: Travel, minimalist living, remote work opportunities

- **Values**: Flexibility, independence, personal growth

- **Pain Points**: Struggling to find consistent work that supports a nomadic lifestyle

With personas like Sarah, you're no longer shooting arrows in the dark—you're hitting *bullseyes*.

Market Research Techniques: Digging Deep

There's a *plethora* of tools and techniques available for conducting market research. Here's a quick run-through of some of the most effective:

1. **Surveys and Questionnaires**: Simple but powerful. Use tools like Google Forms or SurveyMonkey to gather insights directly from your audience. Ask them about their preferences, challenges, and desires. You can go directly into relevant Facebook groups or Reddit and ask your "ideal customers" what problems they are facing, what would help them the most, or what their ultimate goals are.

2. **Social Media Listening**: Tools like Hootsuite, Buffer, Ask-

thePublic or even native social media insights can provide a treasure trove of information. Listen to conversations, check in the comments for feedback, track hashtags, and see which content resonates most with your followers.

3. **Competitor Analysis**: Check out what your competitors are doing. What's working for them? What's missing? Tools like SEMrush and Ahrefs can provide competitive insights into keywords, content performance, and social media strategies.

4. **Customer Reviews and Feedback**: Dive into reviews on website, social media, and even competitors' pages. Reviews are windows into your customers' minds, revealing what they love and what they loathe.

Embracing Data with CRM Systems

If you're serious about understanding your market, a Customer Relationship Management (CRM) system is your new best friend. Platforms like , Salesforce, HubSpot, or Zoho CRM can aggregate customer data, track interactions, and segment your audience for more personalized communication.

Imagine having at your fingertips a detailed history of every interaction a persona like Sarah has had with your brand. From the emails she's opened to the links she's clicked, and the products she's bought, this data is invaluable in crafting highly targeted campaigns that speak directly to her needs and aspirations.

Keep Evolving: Market Trends and Adaptability

The online world is ever-changing, and so is your audience. Trends change, new technologies emerge, and consumer preferences shift. Staying ahead of the curve means *constantly* revisiting and updating your market understanding.

Set regular intervals to revisit your customer personas and market data. Did Sarah shift from freelance work to launching her own digital agency? Did she start using a new social media platform? Adapting to these changes ensures that your marketing efforts remain relevant and impactful.

Action Steps for Understanding Your Market:

1. **Define Your Demographics**: Collect data on age, gender, income level, location, etc.

2. **Dive into Psychographics**: Understand lifestyle, values, interests, and behavioral traits.

3. **Create Customer Personas**: Develop detailed, fictional profiles of your ideal customers.

4. **Conduct Market Research**: Utilize surveys, social media listening, competitor analysis, and reviews.

5. **Leverage CRM Systems**: Use tools to gather and analyze customer data.

6. **Stay Updated**: Regularly review and update your market understanding.

Understanding your market is not a one-time task but an ongoing journey. It's about painting a vivid picture of your audience and continuously refining it with fresh data and insights. This foundational knowledge will guide every aspect of your sales strategy, from content creation to closing deals.

Ready to dive deeper into this journey? Trust me, this is *just the beginning*. **Buckle up,** because we're about to take your online sales game to blissful heights!

2

Building Your Irresistible Online Presence

Crafting Your Digital Fortress

Alright, you online sensation, it's time to establish your online presence—a digital fortress where your audience finds not just products but an *experience*, a community, and a brand they can't get enough of. In today's marketplace, your online presence is your storefront, business card, and first impression all rolled into one dazzling package. So, it's got to be impeccable!

Think of your online presence as your superhero costume. It's got to be authentic, powerful, and unmistakably YOU. Every post, picture, tweet, and email should reflect your brand's essence and resonate with your audience. Let's break it down step-by-step.

Step 1: Choosing the Right Social Media Platforms

First things first, you need to decide where to roam. Not all social media platforms are created equal, and not all will serve your business goals. Don't spread yourself too thin by trying to be everywhere—focus on where your audience hangs out.

Here's the lowdown on some of the big players:

- **Facebook**: Ideal for community building and detailed targeting with ads. Great for longer content and engaging with a broad audience.

- **Instagram**: Perfect for visual storytelling. Ideal for brands with strong visual content—think photography, fashion, food, and lifestyle.

- **LinkedIn**: The go-to for B2B connections. A must for professionals, thought leadership, and networking. Tends to bring in a high level customer base.

- **Twitter**: Excellent for quick updates, engagement with trending topics, and customer service.

- **TikTok**: The rising star for reaching younger audiences through short, engaging videos.

- **Youtube**: The search engine of all all DIY'ers, self-educators, and anyone attempting to learn a new skill. Great for long-form content and really letting your customer get to know you.

Choose wisely, and remember: it's about quality over quantity. Focus on where you can make the most impact.

Step 2: Creating a Professional and Engaging Profile

Your social media profile is your digital handshake. It's your first impression—or your "elevator pitch"—condensed into a glance. Here's how to make it count:

- **Profile Picture**: Use a high-quality, professional photo or logo. Make sure it's consistent across platforms so your audience instantly recognizes you.

- **Username and Handle**: Keep it simple, memorable, and aligned with your brand. If possible, add relevant keywords into your username to help you rank in search terms.

- **Bio**: Craft a captivating bio that tells people who you are, what you do, and why they should care. Include a sprinkle of personality! If you can direct people to click on your bio link by offering a freebie, even better.

- **Contact Info**: Make it easy for people to reach you. Include your email, business phone number, directions to DM you or comment, or a link to a contact form. If you're having a hard time keeping up with comments and DM's you can utilize an auto-responder that will send you customers information based on a word or phase they comment.

- **Link**: Utilize the link in your bio to drive traffic to your most important page—whether it's your website, a landing page, or your latest campaign.

Step 3: Consistency is Key

Consistency breeds familiarity, and familiarity breeds trust. Ensure that your branding—logos, colors, fonts, and messaging—is consistent across all platforms. This helps create a cohesive brand experience:

- **Visuals**: Use a consistent color palette and style. Your posts should look like they belong to the same family.

- **Voice**: Develop a signature voice that reflects your brand's personality. Whether it's witty, professional, or laid-back, keep it consistent.

- **Posting Schedule**: Be consistent with your posting schedule. Whether it's daily, bi-weekly, or weekly, stick to it. Tools like Hootsuite or Buffer can help you plan and schedule posts in advance.

Step 4: Crafting Killer Content

Content is king, queen, and everything in between. Your goal is to create content that does more than just fill a feed—it should *captivate, inform, and inspire* **action**.

- **Educational Content**: Share tips, how-tos, tutorials, and industry insights. Prove you're not just another pretty face online—you're an authority.

- **Engaging Content**: Post questions, polls, and challenges that encourage audience interaction. Spark conversations and build a community.

- **Emotional Content**: Share stories, testimonials, and behind-the-scenes looks. Be authentic and relatable—show there's a human behind the brand.

- **Visual Content**: Invest in high-quality images, videos, and graphics. Use tools like Canva for professional-looking visuals.

- **Value-Driven Content**: Ensure every piece of content provides value—whether it's solving a problem, entertaining, or offering a new perspective.

Step 5: Engaging with Your Audience

An irresistible online presence isn't a one-way street—it's built on engagement. Respond to comments, messages, and reviews promptly. Show genuine interest in your audience's thoughts, questions, and feedback. Think of your audience not as numbers but as individuals with whom you're building relationships.

- **Replies and Comments**: Take time to respond thoughtfully. Show appreciation for positive feedback and address concerns with empathy and solutions.

- **Live Interactions**: Host live Q&A sessions, webinars, or real-time updates to foster real-time interactions.

- **User-Generated Content**: Encourage your audience to create content related to your brand. Share and celebrate their posts and stories.

Step 6: Using Analytics to Refine Your Strategy

Tracking your performance allows you to see what's working and what's not. Most social platforms provide insightful analytics—make good use of them.

- **Engagement Rates**: Monitor likes, shares, comments, and saves. Engagement metrics reveal how well your audience is connecting with your content.

- **Reach and Impressions**: Track how many people are seeing your posts and how often. This helps gauge your content's visibility.

- **Click-Through Rates (CTR)**: Measure how many people click on your links. High CTR means your posts are driving traffic effectively.

- **Conversions**: Ultimately, track how many of these interactions lead to the desired actions (like purchases, sign-ups, or inquiries).

Action Steps for Building Your Online Presence

1. **Choose Your Platforms**: Focus on the social media platforms that best align with your audience and goals.

2. **Optimize Your Profile**: Create a professional, engaging, and consistent profile across all platforms.

3. **Be Consistent**: Ensure visual and voice consistency and maintain a regular posting schedule.

4. **Create Valuable Content**: Develop a mix of educational, engaging, emotional, visual, and value-driven content.

5. **Engage with Your Audience**: Respond to interaction, foster engagement, and build relationships.

6. **Analyze and Refine**: Use analytics to track performance and refine your strategy.

Building an irresistible online presence isn't about overnight success; it's about daily, *consistent* efforts that show up, engage, and deliver value over time. As you implement these steps, you'll cultivate a digital presence that not only attracts but also converts and retains customers. Ready to build that digital fortress? Let's gear up and make it happen!

3

Crafting Your Value Proposition

The Heartbeat of Your Sales Strategy

Welcome back, heavy hitter! Now that you've laid a solid foundation with your understanding of the market and built a magnetic online presence, it's time to dive into what will become the *heartbeat* of your sales strategy—your **Unique Value Proposition** (UVP). This is the magic sauce that sets you apart from the sea of competitors and makes customers choose you time and time again.

Picture this: Your UVP is like a beacon that shines a spotlight on you and screams, "Hey, look over here! I've got exactly what you need!" It's what tells your audience why they should care about what you're offering and why they should pick you over anyone else. Crafting a compelling UVP isn't just about being clever—it's about being clear, specific, and true to your brand's essence.

The Anatomy of a Compelling UVP

Your UVP should be like a well-crafted masterpiece, where every word is chosen *carefully* to convey maximum impact.

Here are the core components you'll need:

- **Headline**: Grab their attention. This should be a clear statement of the end benefit you're offering.

- **Subheadline or 2-3 Sentence Paragraph**: Expand on the headline. Explain what you offer, who it's for, and why it's valuable.

- **Key Benefits/Features**: Bullet-point the core benefits or features. Make it scannable.

- **Visual Element**: Optional but powerful. A strong image or graphic can reinforce your message.

Step 1: Identify Your Ideal Customer's Pain Points

Before you can craft a UVP, you need raw materials—real insights from your target audience about their struggles, desires, and pain points. This is where those personas we created in Chapter 1 come in handy. What keeps them up at night? What problems are they desperate to solve? Your UVP should be directly tied to alleviating their biggest pains or fulfilling their deepest desires.

Step 2: Highlight What Makes You Different

Next, pinpoint what differentiates you from the competition. What do you offer that no one else does? It could be:
- A unique feature of your product.
- Superior customer service.
- Exclusive content or experiences.
- A strong brand story or mission.

Remember, the goal is to be unique, not just better. It's about providing something your competitors don't or can't.

Step 3: Combine Specificity with Benefits

Your UVP should balance specificity ("what" exactly you're offering) with benefits (the "so what"—how it helps the customer).

Let's look at an example:

- **Specificity**: "We offer 24/7 customer support."

- **Benefit**: "Because you should have peace of mind no matter what time it is."

<u>**Combined UVP**</u>: "Around-the-clock customer support so you can have peace of mind, 24/7."

Step 4: Make It Clear and Concise

Clarity *trumps* cleverness. Your UVP should be easy to understand at a glance. Avoid jargon and complex language. Remember, you want your audience to immediately grasp what you're offering and why it matters to them.

Step 5: Test and Refine

Once you've crafted your UVP, don't set it in stone. Test it out. Use surveys, A/B testing, and feedback from your audience to see how it lands. Does it resonate? Does it compel action? Be prepared to tweak and refine it based on real-world feedback.

Real-World Examples

Here are a few examples of effective UVPs that cut through the noise:

1. **Slack**: "Be More Productive at Work with Less Effort"

    a. **Headline**: "Be More Productive at Work with Less Effort

    b. **Subheadline**: "Slack brings all your communication together in one simple place."

    c. **Benefits**: Simplified team communication, centralized information, your team is more productive.

2. **Dollar Shave Club**: "A Great Shave for a Few Bucks a Month"

    a. **Headline**: "A Great Shave for a Few Bucks a Month"

    b. **Subheadline**: "Dollar Shave Club delivers amazing razors and grooming products for just a few bucks."

    c. **Benefits**: Affordable, convenient delivery, high-quality products.

3. **Trello**: "Organize Anything, Together"

   a. **Headline**: "Organize Anything, Together"

   b. **Subheadline**: "Trello lets you work more collaboratively and get more done."

   c. **Benefits**: Collaborative project management, customizable organization tools, boosts productivity.

Action Steps for Crafting Your UVP:

1. **Dig Deep into Customer Pain Points**: Revisit your customer personas and identify their biggest challenges or desires.

2. **Identify Your Unique Differentiators**: What do you offer that no one else can?

3. **Combine Specificity with Benefits**: Clearly articulate what you do and why it matters.

4. **Keep It Clear and Concise**: Avoid jargon and complex language.

5. **Test and Refine**: Use real-world feedback to tweak and perfect your UVP.

Your UVP is the ***cornerstone*** of your entire sales strategy. It's a powerful tool that, when executed correctly, can transform your marketing efforts and set you miles apart from the competition. By understanding your audience's deepest needs and crafting a UVP that speaks directly to those needs, you're not just selling a product or service—you're providing a solution they can't resist.

Ready to make your UVP the headline act of your marketing show? **Let's get to work**, and let your value shine!

If you're a little overwhelmed and not quite sure how to get these tasks accomplished in Part I, I have a step by step training that we discuss in Chapter 17 that will walk you through these exercises and comes with 300 chat gpt prompts to help automate some of this research!

Part II

Mastering Content Creation & Engagement

4

Content is King

The Power of High-Quality Content

It's time to talk about content—the *lifeblood* of your online presence. You've heard the saying "Content is king," but in the bustling digital realm, content is not just king; it's the *entire* royal court. From captivating visuals to compelling narratives, your content is what draws people in, keeps them engaged, and motivates them to take action.

In this chapter, we'll unlock the secrets to creating high-quality content that doesn't just fill space but commands attention and drives results. Ready to transform your content strategy? Let's dive in!

Crafting Your Content Strategy

Creating clutter isn't the goal. Creating **value** is. An *exceptional* content strategy stems from a deep understanding of your audience (thanks to Chapters 1-3!) and a structured plan that aligns with your business objectives.

1. **Define Your Goals**: What do you want your content to achieve? Brand awareness? Lead generation? Customer retention? Define clear, measurable goals.

2. **Identify Your Audience's Needs**: Refer back to your customer personas. What questions are they asking? What problems are they facing?

3. **Content Types and Formats**: Blogs, videos, infographics, emails, social media posts, podcasts—the variety is endless. Choose formats that best suit your message and audience preferences.

4. **Content Calendar**: Plan your content in advance. A content calendar helps you stay organized and ensures a consistent flow of content. Tools like Trello or Google Sheets can be invaluable here.

The Elements of Engaging Content

Creating content that clicks (both literally and figuratively) involves more than just slapping words on a page or images on a feed. Here's what you need to make your content truly engaging:

1. **Relevance and Value**: Content that's relevant to your audience's needs and interests will **always** win. Provide insights, solve problems, or entertain—just make sure it's worth their time.

2. **Eye-Catching Visuals**: Humans are visual creatures. Use high-quality images, graphics, and videos to break up text and add visual appeal. Canva is a fantastic tool for creating professional-looking visuals.

3. **Compelling Headlines**: Your headline is the first thing people see. Make it catchy, clear, and compelling. Use numbers, questions, or powerful adjectives to draw attention.

4. **Storytelling**: People crave stories. Whether it's a customer success story, your brand's journey, or a behind-the-scenes look—stories create emotional connections and make your content memorable.

5. **Calls-to-Action (CTAs)**: Every piece of content should have a purpose. Include clear CTAs that guide your audience to the next step, whether it's subscribing to a newsletter, downloading a resource, or making a purchase.

Optimizing for SEO

Search Engine Optimization (SEO) is crucial for ensuring your content gets found. Here are some SEO fundamentals to keep in mind:

1. **Keyword Research**: Use tools like Google Keyword Planner, Ahrefs, or SEMrush to find keywords your audience is searching for. Incorporate these naturally into your content.

2. **On-Page SEO:** Optimize titles, meta descriptions, headers, and images. Ensure your content is structured and easy to

read.

3. **Quality and Length**: Longer content tends to rank better, but quality trumps quantity. Aim for comprehensive, well-researched content that provides real value.

4. **Link Building**: Include internal links to other relevant content on your site and external links to authoritative sources. Encourage backlinks from other sites.

Leveraging Different Content Types

Let's explore some popular content types and how to maximize their impact:

1. **Blog Posts**: Keep them informative, engaging, and SEO-optimized. Use a mix of listicles, how-tos, and opinion pieces. Regularly update your blog to keep it fresh and relevant.

2. **Social Media Posts**: Tailor content to suit each platform. Use Instagram for visual storytelling, Twitter for quick updates, LinkedIn for professional insights, and Facebook for community engagement.

3. **Videos**: Videos are incredibly engaging. Create tutorials, product demos, live streams, vlogs, and testimonials. Focus on quality production, clear messaging, and captivating visuals.

4. **Infographics**: Use infographics to simplify complex infor-

mation and make it visually appealing. They're great for sharing on social media and can drive traffic back to your site.

5. **Emails**: Create personalized, targeted emails that nurture leads and convert subscribers into customers. Segment your email list and provide value-rich content tailored to each segment.

6. **Podcasts**: Podcasts are a fantastic way to share in-depth insights and connect with your audience on a personal level. Plan episodes that offer value and engage your listeners.

Analyzing and Iterating

Content creation is not a set-it-and-forget-it process. Continually analyze your content's performance and make data-driven decisions to improve:

1. **Engagement Metrics**: Track likes, shares, comments, time on page, and bounce rates to gauge how your audience is interacting with your content.

2. **Conversion Metrics**: Monitor click-through rates, downloads, sign-ups, and sales to understand how well your content is converting.

3. **Feedback**: Pay attention to audience feedback. Use surveys, polls, and direct messages to gather insights and improve your content strategy.

4. **Continuous Improvement:** Use analytics tools like Google Analytics, Facebook Insights, TikTok Analytics and email marketing platforms to track performance. Regularly revisit and adjust your content strategy based on what's working and what's not.

Action Steps for Crafting High-Quality Content:

---

1. **Define Your Content Goals**: Identify what you want your content to achieve.

2. **Understand Your Audience**: Tailor your content to their needs and interests.

3. **Create a Content Calendar**: Plan and schedule your content in advance.

4. **Optimize for SEO**: Incorporate keywords, optimize on-page elements, and build links.

5. **Diverse Content Types**: Mix blogs, videos, infographics, social media posts, and more.

6. **Engage and Convert**: Use compelling visuals, storytelling, CTAs, and personalized emails.

7. **Analyze and Improve**: Regularly track performance and adjust your strategy.

Creating high-quality content is both an art and a science. With the right strategy, your content will *captivate* your audience, drive engagement, and boost your online sales. Ready to take your content game to the next level? Let's get to work and make your content **reign** supreme!

5

Social Media Marketing Techniques

Unleashing the Power of Social Media

You're already becoming a super savvy marketer! Now that we've covered content creation, it's time to leverage the *incredible* power of social media to amplify your reach and drive those coveted online sales. Social media isn't just a platform for cat videos and food photos (though we love those too)—it's a dynamic ecosystem where brands can thrive, engage deeply with their audience, and convert interest into revenue.

In this chapter, we're going to dive into platform-specific strategies, engagement tactics, and analytics to help you master the world of social media marketing. Ready to turn those likes and shares into loyal customers? Let's go!

Platform-Specific Strategies

Every social media platform has its unique characteristics and ways to engage with users. Let's break down some of the major players:

1. ***Facebook***: Facebook is a powerhouse for building communities and running targeted ad campaigns. Here's how to make the most of it:

    a. **Creating a Business Page**: Start with a well-optimized business page. Include a clear cover photo, detailed 'About' section, and contact info.

    b. **Engaging Content**: Post a mix of content—videos, infographics, live sessions, and written posts. Use Facebook Stories for short-lived, engaging content.

    c. **Facebook Groups**: Create or join groups where your target audience hangs out. Engage with group members by sharing valuable insights and resources.

    d. **Advertising**: Facebook Ads are incredibly powerful if used correctly. Utilize Facebook's targeting options to reach specific demographics and interests. Use A/B testing to optimize your ads.

2. ***Instagram***: Instagram is your go-to for visual storytelling and branding. Here's how to shine:

    a. **Profile Optimization**: Use a professional profile photo and clear bio. Include a link to your website or latest campaign.

    b. **High-Quality Visuals**: Focus on high-quality images and videos. Use Instagram Stories, IGTV, and Reels to diversify your content.

    c. **Consistency**: Maintain a consistent aesthetic and posting schedule. Tools like Planoly or Later can help plan your feed.

    d. **Engagement**: Engage with your audience through comments, likes, and direct messages. Use Instagram's interactive features like polls, questions, and quizzes in Stories.

    e. **Hashtags**: Use relevant hashtags to increase your reach. Mix popular and niche hashtags to target your audience effectively.

3. ***LinkedIn***: LinkedIn is crucial for B2B marketing and professional networking and you can draw in a higher level customer from this platform. Here's how to make it work:

    a. **Professional Profile**: Ensure your company profile is professional, including a detailed 'About' section, services, and contact info.

    b. **Thought Leadership**: Share industry insights, thought leadership articles, and company updates. Engage with posts in your network by commenting and sharing.

    c. **Networking**: Connect with industry professionals, potential clients, and partners. Build relationships through meaningful conversations.

    d. **LinkedIn Groups**: Join and participate in LinkedIn Groups relevant to your industry. Share your expertise and resources.

   e. **LinkedIn Ads**: Use LinkedIn Ads for targeted campaigns. Focus on job titles, industries, and company size for precise targeting.

4. ***Twitter***: Twitter is the platform for real-time updates and conversations. Here's how to utilize it:

   a. **Profile Optimization**: Use a recognizable profile picture and a bio that includes keywords and a link to your website.

   b. **Regular Tweets**: Tweet regularly and consistently. Share a mix of content—company updates, industry news, and behind-the-scenes looks.

   c. **Engagement**: Engage with your audience through replies, retweets, and mentions. Jump into relevant conversations and use Twitter Chats for visibility.

   d. **Trending Topics**: Keep an eye on trending topics and hashtags. Join conversations that are relevant to your brand.

   e. **Twitter Ads**: Utilize Twitter Ads for promoted tweets, accounts, and trends. Target based on interests, keywords, and demographics.

5. ***TikTok:*** TikTok is rapidly rising, especially among younger audiences. Here's how to make an impact:

   a. **Creative Content**: Focus on short, engaging, and creative videos. Use popular music, effects, and trends.

b. **Hashtag Challenges**: Participate in or create your own hashtag challenges to boost engagement.

c. **Influencers**: Collaborate with influencers to expand your reach.

d. **TikTok Ads**: Use TikTok Ads to create engaging ad formats like In-Feed Ads, Branded Hashtag Challenges, and Branded Effects.

e. **Community Engagement**: Engage with comments, duets, and collaboration videos.

Engaging with Your Audience

Engagement is the heart of social media marketing. Here's how to foster a thriving online community:

1. **Responsive Interaction**: Always respond to comments, messages, and mentions. Show your audience that you value their interaction.

2. **User-Generated Content**: Encourage your audience to create content related to your brand. Share and celebrate their posts.

3. **Contests and Giveaways**: Host contests and giveaways to boost engagement and reward loyalty. Make participation easy and fun.

4. **Quality Over Quantity**: Focus on the quality of interactions rather than the sheer volume. Meaningful engagements build stronger relationships.

5. **Influencer Partnerships**: Partner with influencers who resonate with your brand values. Influencer endorsements can significantly boost your credibility and reach.

Measuring and Analyzing Performance

Understanding your social media performance helps you refine your strategy. Here's what to track:

1. **Engagement Metrics**: Likes, comments, shares, and saves indicate how well your content resonates with your audience.

2. **Reach and Impressions**: Monitor how many people see your content and how often. This helps gauge visibility and awareness.

3. **Click-Through Rate (CTR)**: Track how many people click on your links. A high CTR is a good indicator of compelling content.

4. **Conversions**: Measure how many social media interactions lead to desired actions like purchases, sign-ups, or inquiries.

5. **Sentiment Analysis**: Evaluate the sentiment of comments and mentions to understand public perception of your brand.

> **Action Steps for Social Media Marketing:**

1. **Choose the Right Platforms**: Focus on social media platforms that best align with your target audience.

2. **Optimize Profiles**: Ensure your profiles are professional and engaging across all platforms.

3. **Create Consistent Content**: Develop a mix of content tailored to each platform. Maintain consistency in posting schedules and visual aesthetics.

4. **Engage Actively**: Respond to interactions, encourage user-generated content, and foster meaningful engagement.

5. **Utilize Ads**: Leverage platform-specific ad tools to run targeted campaigns. Monitor and optimize ad performance.

6. **Track Performance**: Use analytics tools to measure key metrics and refine your strategy based on data.

Mastering social media marketing is about understanding each platform's unique features and tailoring your strategy to engage effectively with your audience. With the right techniques and consistent effort, you'll transform your social media channels into powerful tools for driving online sales and growing your brand.

Get to work turning your social media presence into a sales-generating powerhouse and start watching the likes, comments, shares, and conversions roll in!

6

Email Marketing – The Silent Closer

The Underrated Dynamo of Digital Marketing

While social media often steals the spotlight, email marketing quietly drives some of the highest conversion rates in digital marketing. It's the trusted ally that's always there, ready to deliver your message directly to your audience's inbox.

Think of email marketing as your intimate coffee date with your audience—no distractions, just you and them having a meaningful conversation. In this chapter, we'll explore how to build an effective email list, write compelling emails, and use segmentation and automation to convert leads into loyal customers. In Chapter 17, I explain how you can access 14 days worth of done-for-you high converting email templates. Ready to turn email into your conversion powerhouse? Let's dive in!

Building an Effective Email List

Your email list is one of your most valuable assets. Building it effectively ensures you have a direct line to your audience. Here's how to grow an engaged, high-quality list:

- *Opt-In Forms*

    - **Strategic Placement**: Place opt-in forms on high-traffic pages like your homepage, blog posts, and landing pages. Ensure they're eye-catching but not intrusive.

    - **Value Proposition**: Clearly state what subscribers will get in return for signing up (e.g., exclusive content, discounts, or freebies). Make it irresistible.

    - **Simplicity**: Keep the sign-up form simple. Ask only for essential information—usually just a name and email address.

- *Lead Magnets*

    - **Free Resources**: Offer valuable resources like eBooks, checklists, templates, or webinars in exchange for email addresses. Ensure it solves a specific problem or fulfills a need.

    - **Gated Content**: Lock premium content behind an email opt-in. This could be in-depth guides, video tutorials, or exclusive articles.

- *Social Media Promotion*

    - **Social Campaigns**: Promote your email sign-up on your social media channels. Highlight the benefits of subscribing.

- **Contests and Giveaways**: Host contests or giveaways that require email subscription to enter. This can rapidly grow your list.

* *Partnerships and Collaborations*

    - **Influencers and Affiliates**: Partner with influencers or affiliates who can promote your email list to their audience.
    - **Cross-Promotions**: Collaborate with complementary brands to co-promote email subscriptions, offering joint resources or discounts.

Crafting Compelling Email Content

Once you have your list, it's time to craft emails that your subscribers can't wait to open.

Here's how:

Subject Lines

- **Catchy and Compelling**: Your subject line should grab attention instantly. Use curiosity, urgency, and benefits to entice opens.
- **A/B Testing**: Test different subject lines to see what res-

onates. Small tweaks can significantly affect open rates.

Personalization

- **Use Their Name**: Personalize your emails by using the recipient's name. It creates a sense of connection.
- **Segmented Content**: Tailor the email content based on subscriber behavior, interests, and demographics. The more relevant, the better.

Engage and Provide Value

- **Content Variety**: Mix up the content to keep it interesting—newsletters, product updates, behind-the-scenes looks, educational content, and special offers.
- **Storytelling**: Engage your readers with compelling stories. Share customer success stories, brand narratives, and relatable anecdotes.
- **Visual Appeal**: Use high-quality images, graphics, and a clean layout. Tools like Canva can help create beautiful email templates.

Clear Call to Action (CTA)

- **Define the Goal**: Every email should have a clear goal—whether it's clicking a link, signing up for a webinar, or making a purchase.

- **Strong CTAs**: Use strong, action-oriented language for your CTAs. Make them stand out visually.

***

Segmentation and Automation

Segmentation and automation turn good email marketing into great email marketing. Here's how to use them effectively:

1. **Segmentation**

    a. **Demographic Segmentation**: Group subscribers based on age, gender, location, or job title. Send tailored content that speaks directly to them.

    b. **Behavioral Segmentation**: Segment based on subscriber actions—like previous purchases, website behavior, or email engagement.

    c. **Interest-Based Segmentation**: Group subscribers by their interests or preferences indicated during sign-up or through previous interactions.

2. **Automation**

    a. **Welcome Series**: Automate a series of emails that introduce new subscribers to your brand, highlight key products or services, and set expectations.

b. **Abandoned Cart Emails**: Recover lost sales by sending automated follow-ups to customers who left items in their shopping cart.

c. **Post-Purchase Emails**: Enhance the customer experience with automated emails post-purchase—thanking them, offering usage tips, or suggesting complementary products.

d. **Re-Engagement Campaigns**: Use automation to reach out to inactive subscribers with special offers or enticing content to win them back.

3. **Analyzing Email Marketing Performance:** Tracking performance metrics allows you to refine your strategy continuously. Here are key metrics to monitor:

   a. **Click-Through Rates (CTR)**: Measures the percentage of subscribers who clicked on a link within your email. High CTRs indicate engaging content and strong CTAs.

   b. **Conversion Rates**: Track how many subscribers took the desired action—whether it's making a purchase, signing up for a webinar, or filling out a form.

   c. **Bounce Rates**: Monitor the percentage of emails that couldn't be delivered. A high bounce rate could indicate issues with your email list quality.

   d. **Unsubscribe Rates**: Keep an eye on how many people

are unsubscribing. This can provide insights into how well your content is being received.

> **Action Steps for Effective Email Marketing:**

1. **Build Your List**: Use opt-in forms, lead magnets, social media, and collaborations to grow your email list.

2. **Craft Compelling Emails**: Focus on catchy subject lines, personalized content, engaging storytelling, and strong CTAs.

3. **Segment and Automate**: Use segmentation to tailor content and automation to nurture relationships and drive conversions.

4. **Monitor Performance**: Track key metrics and refine your strategy based on data insights.

Email marketing remains one of the most powerful tools at your disposal for closing sales and building long-term customer relationships. By focusing on building a quality list, crafting compelling and personalized content, leveraging segmentation and automation, and continuously analyzing performance, you'll transform your email campaigns into silent but powerful closers. Let's get those emails flying and those conversions soaring!

Part III

THE ART & SCIENCE OF SELLING

7

The Psychology of Selling

Unleashing the Power of the Mind

Sales isn't just a transaction; it's a profound dance of human interaction deeply rooted in psychology. Understanding the mind of your buyer—their desires, fears, and motivations—gives you the golden keys to unlock consistent sales success. When you master the psychology of selling, you're not just selling a product; you're *solving a problem*, fulfilling a need, and making a meaningful connection.

In this chapter, we'll explore the psychological principles that drive buying decisions and how to leverage these insights to create compelling sales strategies. Ready to channel your inner mentalist and decode the mind of your buyers? Let's dive in!

Understanding Buyer Behavior

At its core, selling is about understanding and influencing behavior. Here are some fundamental psychological principles that affect buying decisions:

The Need for Social Proof

People tend to follow the actions of others, especially in uncertain situations. Social proof includes testimonials, reviews, ratings, and endorsements that validate your credibility:

- **Testimonials**: Showcase positive feedback from satisfied customers.

- **Reviews and Ratings**: Highlight high ratings and favorable reviews.

- **Influencer Endorsements**: Partner with influencers who resonate with your brand.

- **User-Generated Content**: Encourage and share content created by your customers using your products.

The Principle of Reciprocity

Human beings naturally feel compelled to return favors. When you give something of value, people often feel a sense of obligation to reciprocate:

- **Free Resources**: Offer free eBooks, webinars, or templates.

- **Exclusive Discounts**: Give special discounts to subscribers or loyal customers.

- **Personalized Experiences**: Provide a highly personalized customer experience.

The Scarcity Principle

Limited availability often increases value perception and urgency. Scarcity creates a fear of missing out (FOMO):

- **Limited-Time Offers**: Create time-sensitive promotions and flash sales.

- **Exclusive Products**: Offer limited-edition products or services.

- **Countdown Timers**: Use countdown timers in emails and on landing pages.

The Anchoring Effect

People heavily rely on the first piece of information (the anchor) when making decisions. Anchoring can significantly influence perception:

- **Initial Pricing**: Present a higher initial price, then offer a discount or a lower-cost option.

- **Package Deals**: Show a premium package first to make standard or basic options seem more appealing.

Authority and Credibility

People trust and follow authoritative figures. Establishing yourself as an expert or credible source can significantly boost sales:

- **Credentials**: Highlight your qualifications, awards, and certifications.

- **Content Marketing**: Consistently produce high-quality, informative content.

- **Public Speaking**: Engage in public speaking opportunities and webinars.

Building Trust and Rapport

Trust is the cornerstone of any successful sales relationship. Here's how to build genuine trust and rapport with your prospects:

Active Listening

Listening is more than just hearing words; it's about understanding the underlying emotions and needs:

- **Reflective Listening**: Repeat back what the prospect says to show understanding and empathy.

- **Open-Ended Questions**: Ask questions that encourage detailed responses, giving you deeper insights.

Transparency and Honesty

Be honest and transparent about what you're offering. Prospects can sense dishonesty, and it can erode trust instantly:

- **Honest Pricing**: Be upfront about costs and any additional fees.

- **Set Realistic Expectations**: Don't overpromise and underdeliver. Be clear about what your product or service can realistically achieve.

Building Rapport

People buy from those they like and trust. Building rapport creates a genuine connection:

- **Finding Common Ground**: Look for shared interests or experiences.

- **Mirroring**: Subtly mimic the prospect's tone, language, and body language to create subconscious alignment.

- **Personalized Interaction**: Address the prospect by name and personalize your communication to make it feel unique.

Leveraging Emotional Triggers

Human decisions are often influenced by emotions more than logic. Here's how to tap into emotional triggers to drive sales:

1. *Fear:* Fear of missing out, fear of loss, and fear of failure are potent motivators:

    a. **Urgency**: Create urgency with limited-time offers and low-stock alerts.

    b. **Risk Reversal**: Offer money-back guarantees to alleviate the fear of making a wrong decision.

2. *Aspiration:* Tap into your prospect's aspirations and dreams:

    a. **Success Stories**: Share testimonials and case studies that showcase success stories.

    b. **Before-and-After**: Highlight transformations and positive outcomes your product or service can deliver.

3. *Belonging:* Humans crave connection and a sense of belonging:

    a. **Community Building**: Create a community around your brand where customers feel connected.

    b. **Inclusive Messaging**: Use inclusive language and imagery to make prospects feel they're part of something bigger.

4. *Pleasure:* Show how your product or service can bring joy, satisfaction, or convenience:

    a. **Positive Imagery**: Use visuals that evoke positive emotions.

  b. **Customer Experience**: Deliver an exceptional customer experience that delights and satisfies.

Overcoming Objections

Handling objections is a crucial part of the sales process. Here's how to address common objections effectively:

1. *Price:* Many objections revolve around cost. Address this by demonstrating value:

  a. **Break Down Value**: Explain the benefits and ROI your product or service provides.

  b. **Offer Payment Plans**: Provide flexible payment options to make the price more manageable.

2. *Skepticism:* Some prospects might doubt your claims. Overcome skepticism with social proof and demonstrations:

  a. **Showcase Testimonials**: Highlight positive feedback and reviews from real customers.

  b. **Provide Demos**: Offer live demos or trials to let prospects experience the product firsthand.

3. *Timing:* Prospects often hesitate due to timing concerns. Address this with urgency and understanding:

  a. **Create Urgency**: Highlight limited-time offers or

bonuses.

b. **Be Flexible**: Offer flexible terms or future scheduling options.

Action Steps for Mastering the Psychology of Selling:

1. **Understand Behavior**: Master psychological principles like social proof, reciprocity, scarcity, and authority.

2. **Build Trust**: Focus on active listening, transparency, and building rapport.

3. **Leverage Emotions**: Tap into fear, aspiration, belonging, and pleasure.

4. **Overcome Objections**: Address common objections with value demonstrations and empathy.

Mastering the psychology of selling *transforms* you from a mere salesperson into a trusted advisor. By understanding and applying these psychological principles, you'll connect with your audience on a deeper level, build lasting relationships, and drive consistent sales success.

8

Mastering the Close: In Videos

The Pinnacle of the Sales Journey

Welcome to the *climax* of the sales journey, where all your hard work and strategic efforts converge—the close. Closing a sale is a **skill** that combines finesse, timing, and understanding buyer psychology. It's not just about sealing the deal; it's about doing so in a way that leaves the customer feeling proud and thrilled about their decision.

In this chapter, we'll explore closing techniques and strategies specifically tailored for selling through videos on platforms like TikTok, where direct interaction with the viewer isn't possible. Ready to become a closing maestro in the video content era?

The Art of the Close: Techniques and Strategies for Video

Crafting a compelling close in a video requires creativity and clarity. Here are some effective techniques adapted for video content:

1. ***The Assumptive Close:*** In video content, you can imply that the viewer will make the purchase by confidently steering them towards the desired action.

    a. **Example**: "When you get your hands on this product, you'll wonder how you ever lived without it. Click the link in my bio to get yours today!"

    b. **Execution**: Use visuals or on-screen text to reinforce the assumed action. Highlight the product in use and its benefits.

2. ***The Urgency Close:*** Creating a sense of urgency through video can prompt quick action. This technique leverages time-sensitive offers.

    a. **Example**: "This exclusive discount is only available for the next 24 hours! Don't miss out—click the link now!"

    b. **Execution**: Incorporate countdown timers or on-screen text indicating the limited time offer. Use fast-paced music to enhance the sense of urgency.

3. ***The Summary Close:*** Summarize the key benefits quickly and end with a strong call-to-action.

    a. **Example**: "With this product, you get [Benefit 1], [Benefit 2], and [Benefit 3]. Ready to transform your life? Tap the link in my bio to order now!"

    b. **Execution**: Use bullet points or icons to highlight benefits visually. End with a clear, direct call-to-action prominently displayed on-screen.

4. ***The Question Close:*** Ask a rhetorical question that nudges the viewer towards the desired action.

    a. **Example**: "Looking for a solution that fits your busy lifestyle? This is it. Click the link and make the change today!"

    b. **Execution**: Use engaging visuals and relatable scenarios. Pose the question directly to the camera, making eye contact to enhance connection.

5. ***The Option Close:*** Presenting options in a video can help narrow the viewer's focus and prompt a decision.

    a. **Example**: "Whether you need the basic or premium version, we've got the perfect solution for you. Choose your option and click the link to buy now."

    b. **Execution**: Show side-by-side comparisons of the options, highlighting the unique features of each. Use clear labels and arrows to direct attention.

6. ***The Financial Close:*** Align the purchase with the viewer's financial benefit or budget considerations.

    a. **Example**: "Investing in this product pays for itself within months. Ready to see how it can save you money? Click the link to learn more and buy today!"

b. **Execution**: Use on-screen text to break down the cost savings or ROI. Incorporate testimonials or case studies to reinforce the financial benefits.

Overcoming Objections in Video

Addressing potential objections in your video content can preemptively alleviate viewer concerns. Here are strategies for common objections:

1. *The "Too Expensive" Objection*

    a. **Value Justification**: Break down the product's benefits and ROI. Use visuals to reinforce long-term savings or earnings.

    b. **Example**: "Worried about the cost? This product saves you money in the long run. Here's how… [Visual Breakdown]. Get yours by clicking the link now!"

2. *The "Not Interested" Objection*

    a. **Re-engage Interest**: Highlight unique benefits and engage with compelling visuals.

    b. **Example**: "Think this isn't for you? Check out what makes this product stand out. [Show Unique Features] Click the link in my bio to learn more!"

3. *The "Need to Think About It" Objection*

    a. **Create Urgency**: Introduce a time-sensitive offer.

b. **Example**: "Still on the fence? Don't wait too long—this offer ends soon! Order now and see the difference for yourself. [Visual Countdown Timer]"

Creating a Sense of Urgency in Video

Urgency in video can drive viewers to act immediately. Here's how to effectively create urgency:

1. ***Scarcity:*** Highlight limited availability to create a fear of missing out (FOMO).

    a. **Example**: "Hurry—only a few left in stock! Click the link to secure yours before they're gone!"

    b. **Execution**: Use on-screen text or voiceover to emphasize scarcity. Include visuals of dwindling stock numbers.

2. ***Time-Limited Offers:*** Leverage time-sensitive discounts or promotions.

    a. **Example**: "For the next 24 hours only, get 20% off! Don't miss out—click the link now!"

    b. **Execution**: Include countdown timers and fast-paced transitions to create urgency.

3. ***Event-Based Urgency:*** Align offers with specific events or milestones.

    a. **Example**: "Celebrate our anniversary with an exclusive deal! Click the link to grab your discount before it's too late!"

   b. **Execution**: Use festive visuals and celebratory music to enhance the sense of occasion.

4. ***Personalized Follow-Ups:*** Personalize in-video messages to create urgency specific to the viewer's potential needs.

   a. **Example**: "I know you've been looking for a solution like this. Act now and get an exclusive bonus! Click the link in my bio!"

   b. **Execution**: Speak directly to the camera using a personalized tone. Use on-screen text to reinforce the special offer.

Closing with Confidence in Video

Closing with confidence means displaying certainty and enthusiasm that resonates through the screen. Here's how to maintain composure and confidence in your videos:

1. ***Positive Body Language:*** Maintain open, confident body language. Make direct eye contact with the camera to create a sense of connection.

2. ***Clear and Concise Communication:*** Be clear, concise, and direct in your closing statements. Avoid over-explaining or hesitant language.

3. ***Empathy and Understanding:*** Show empathy and understanding without appearing desperate. Address concerns

genuinely and positively.

4. ***Practice and Preparation:*** Rehearse your closing lines and be prepared for various scenarios. Preparation breeds confidence.

Action Steps for Mastering the Close in Video Content:

1. **Choose the Right Technique**: Select closing techniques that align with your video's structure and your audience's behavior.

2. **Overcome Objections**: Address common objections using visuals, clear communication, and value demonstrations.

3. **Create Urgency**: Use on-screen text, voiceovers, and engaging visuals to create a sense of urgency.

4. **Close with Confidence**: Maintain positive body language, clear communication, empathy, and thorough preparation.

Mastering the close in video content is about combining strategic techniques with engaging visuals and confident communication. By refining these skills, you'll transform interested viewers into enthusiastic customers, driving your sales success to new heights.

9

Mastering the Close: In Person, Lives & Over the Phone

Overcoming Objections in Real-Time: Phone, In Person, and Live Social Media

When selling over the phone, in person, or during live social media sessions, you're in real-time with your prospect, presenting both a challenge and an opportunity. You need to be quick on your feet, empathetic, and persuasive. Here's how to overcome objections effectively in these scenarios:

The "Too Expensive" Objection

<u>Phone:</u>

- **Empathy and Understanding**: Acknowledge their concern genuinely. "I understand that cost is an important factor for you."
- **Value Highlight**: Break down the value and benefits, potentially using analogies to simplify the comparison. "Think of it as an investment that pays for itself within a few months due to [specific savings/benefits]. Can you see how this could be beneficial in the long run?"

In Person:

- **Body Language**: Use open and confident body language. Address their concern directly while maintaining eye contact.
- **Tangible Demonstration**: If possible, show them the product in action, highlighting its key benefits and superior quality. "Let me show you how this feature makes your daily tasks easier and more efficient."

Live Social Media:

- **Real-Time Interaction**: Acknowledge the comment publicly and address it. "Great question about the pricing! Let's talk about the incredible value you get with this product."
- **Demonstrative Examples**: Show live examples of how the product can save them money or provide significant benefits over time. "Look at how [feature] offers [specific savings/benefits], making it well worth the investment."

The "Not Interested" Objection

Phone:

- **Curiosity Questions**: Ask questions to understand their disinterest. "Can you tell me more about what you're looking for? Is there a specific feature or benefit that would change your mind?"
- **Tailored Solution**: Offer a tailored solution based on their responses. "Based on what you've shared, I think you'll find this aspect of our product particularly valuable."

In Person:

- **Visual Aids**: Use brochures, demos, or presentations to capture interest visually.
- **Engaging Story**: Share a compelling success story or testimonial. "I'd like to share how one of our customers, who initially wasn't interested, found this product to be a game-changer."

Live Social Media:

- **Engagement and Polls**: Engage the audience with polls or questions. "I see some of you are unsure. What features would you like to know more about?"

- **Live Testimonials**: Invite satisfied customers to join the live session or share pre-recorded testimonials. "Listen to how [customer name] found success with our product."

The "Need to Think About It" Objection

Phone:

- **Understanding Concerns**: Ask if there are specific concerns causing them to hesitate. "I understand you need time. Is there something specific holding you back? Maybe I can provide more information."
- **Follow-Up Offer**: Offer a follow-up call and create urgency. "How about I send you some additional details and follow up in a couple of days? Remember, the current offer is available only until [specific deadline]."

In Person:

- **Soft Close**: Use a soft close that respects their need for time but also emphasizes urgency. "I completely understand. How about I give you some more information to review? Just keep in mind, the special pricing we discussed is only available until [specific deadline]."
- **Leave-Behind Materials**: Leave behind brochures or samples for them to review and follow up later. "Here's some additional information. I'll reach out in a few days to see if you have any questions."

Live Social Media:

- **Limited-Time Offers**: Emphasize limited-time offers and benefits during the live session. "I know you might need to think about it, but don't forget, this special offer is only available during this live session!"
- **Live Q&A**: Open the floor for a Q&A session to address specific concerns. "What questions can I answer for you right now to help you make an informed decision?"

> ### Integrative Approach: Combining Techniques

Here's how to blend these techniques across different scenarios to ensure effectiveness:

1. **Preparation**: Know your product inside and out. Anticipate common objections and prepare responses in advance.

2. **Real-Time Adaptation**: Be flexible and adaptive. Listen actively and respond accordingly based on the medium—phone, in-person, or live.

3. **Empathy and Patience**: Always approach objections with empathy and patience. Building trust often leads to better long-term relationships.

Mastering the skill of overcoming objections in real-time interactions—whether over the phone, in person, or during live social media sessions—*requires empathy, quick thinking, and clear communication.* By preparing for common objections and knowing how to address them effectively, you'll enhance your ability to close sales and leave a positive, lasting impression on your prospects. You're now ready to handle objections like a pro and turn hesitant prospects into raving customers!

Part IV

SCALING & OPTIMIZATION

10

Turning Leads into Loyal Customers

The Journey from Prospect to Advocate

The journey from lead to loyal customer extends beyond the initial sale. It's about nurturing relationships and creating experiences that turn one-time buyers into *repeat customers*—and loyal advocates for your brand.

In this chapter, we'll explore **effective** lead nurturing techniques, how to implement a seamless customer experience, and strategies for fostering long-term loyalty.

Lead Nurturing Techniques

Lead nurturing is the process of developing long-term relationships with your prospects at every stage of the sales funnel. Here are some essential techniques:

1. Personalized Communication

Tailor your communication to meet the specific needs and interests of each lead.

- **Segmentation**: Segment your leads based on behavior, demographics, and engagement levels. This allows for more targeted, relevant communication.

- **Personalized Emails**: Use their name and reference their specific interests or actions. "Hi [Name], we noticed you're interested in [Product/Service]. Here's something we think you'll love."

2. Educating Leads

Provide valuable and educational content that helps leads understand your product and its benefits.

- **Content Marketing**: Share blog posts, eBooks, webinars, and case studies that address common pain points and showcase solutions.

- **Drip Campaigns**: Implement email sequences that gradually educate and guide leads towards a purchase decision. Start with introductory content and move towards more detailed information.

3. Consistent Follow-Ups

Stay top of mind with timely and consistent follow-up communications.

- **Automated Follow-Ups**: Use CRM tools to automate follow-up emails based on specific triggers like website visits, email opens, or clicks.

- **Personal Touch**: Occasionally mix in personalized calls or messages to show that you value the relationship.

4. Social Proof and Testimonials

Showcase success stories and testimonials to build trust and credibility.

- **Customer Testimonials**: Share success stories and reviews from satisfied customers.
- **Case Studies**: Provide in-depth case studies that highlight how your product or service solved specific problems.

5. Offering Incentives

Encourage leads to take action by offering incentives.

- **Exclusive Discounts**: Offer limited-time discounts to encourage conversions.
- **Free Trials or Samples**: Allow leads to experience your product or service firsthand without a commitment.

Creating a Seamless Customer Experience

Providing an exceptional customer experience ensures that your leads have a positive interaction with your brand at every touchpoint. Here's how to make it seamless:

1. Onboarding Process

Ensure a smooth and welcoming onboarding experience for new customers.

•**Welcome Emails**: Send a warm and informative welcome email outlining what they can expect.

•**Onboarding Guides**: Provide guides, tutorials, and resources to help them get started with your product or service.

2. Consistent Communication

Maintain clear and consistent communication throughout their journey.

•**Regular Updates**: Keep customers informed about new features, updates, and upcoming promotions.

•**Feedback Requests**: Regularly ask for feedback to show that you value their opinion and are committed to improvement.

3. Excellent Customer Support

Offer responsive and helpful customer support to address any issues or questions promptly.

•**Multiple Channels**: Provide support through multiple channels like email, chat, and phone.

•**Proactive Support**: Reach out proactively to check in on their experience and preempt potential issues.

4. Building Relationships

Focus on building long-term relationships rather than just making sales.

•**Personal Touches**: Send personalized thank-you notes, birthday wishes, or exclusive offers to make customers feel valued.

•**Community Engagement**: Create a community around your brand where customers can connect, share, and engage.

Fostering Long-Term Loyalty

Turning customers into loyal advocates involves ongoing engagement and relationship-building. Here are key strategies:

1. Loyalty Programs

Implement a loyalty program to reward repeat customers.

- **Points System**: Offer points for purchases that can be redeemed for discounts or free products.

- **Exclusive Perks**: Provide exclusive perks like early access to new products, special events, or personalized offers.

2. Regular Engagement

Keep customers engaged with your brand through regular, value-added interactions.

- **Content Updates**: Regularly share valuable content like blogs, videos, and newsletters that keep them informed and engaged.

- **Interactive Campaigns**: Run interactive campaigns like contests, challenges, or live Q&A sessions to maintain engagement.

3. Asking for Referrals

Encourage loyal customers to refer friends and family to your brand.

- **Referral Programs**: Create referral programs that offer incentives for both the referrer and the new customer.

- **Easy Sharing**: Make it easy for customers to share their positive experiences with ready-made social media posts or email templates.

4. Soliciting Feedback

Show that you value their input and are committed to improvement.

- **Surveys and Polls**: Regularly solicit feedback through surveys and polls.
- **Actionable Insights**: Act on the feedback received to make tangible improvements, and communicate these changes to your customers.

Action Steps for Turning Leads into Loyal Customers:

---

1. **Nurture Leads**: Use personalized communication, educational content, consistent follow-ups, social proof, and incentives to nurture relationships.

2. **Create a Seamless Experience**: Focus on a smooth onboarding process, consistent communication, excellent support, and relationship-building.

3. **Foster Loyalty**: Implement loyalty programs, maintain regular engagement, encourage referrals, and solicit customer feedback.

Turning leads into loyal customers is about more than just making a sale; it's about developing meaningful relationships and providing exceptional experiences at every stage of the customer journey. By nurturing leads, creating seamless experiences, and fostering long-term loyalty, you'll build a robust base of loyal customers who not only return but also advocate for your brand. I'm so excited for you to start creating amazing experiences and build that true customer loyalty!

11

Automation and Technology

The Engine of Efficient Sales

Welcome, tech-savvy entrepreneur! In the rapidly evolving digital landscape, automation and technology are the catalysts that can propel your sales efforts from good to *extraordinary*. They allow you to streamline processes, nurture leads at scale, and focus your energy on high-impact activities.

In this chapter, we'll delve into the tools and techniques that can help you automate your sales funnel, manage customer relationships effectively, and maximize your efficiency. Ready to turbocharge your sales process with the power of technology?

Automation Tools for Sales and Marketing

To streamline your sales and marketing efforts, you need the right tools. Here's a look at some essential automation tools:

1. Customer Relationship Management (CRM) Systems

A CRM system helps manage interactions with current and potential customers, ensuring a streamlined process from lead generation to closing the sale.
   • **Popular Tools**: Salesforce, HubSpot, Zoho CRM.
   • **Key Features**: Contact management, lead tracking, sales pipeline management, task automation, email integration.

Case Study Example:

A small business using HubSpot CRM saw a 30% increase in lead conversion rates by automating follow-up emails and tracking customer interactions in one centralized platform.

2. Email Marketing Automation

Automated email marketing allows you to nurture leads and engage customers with personalized and timely messages.
   • **Popular Tools**: Mailchimp, ActiveCampaign, ConvertKit.
   • **Key Features**: Drip campaigns, triggered emails, segmentation, A/B testing, analytics.

Case Study Example:

A startup leveraged Mailchimp's automation features to send personalized onboarding sequences to new subscribers, resulting in a 25% increase in engagement and a 20% boost in conversions.

3. Social Media Management Tools

Managing multiple social media accounts can be overwhelming. Social media management tools help schedule posts, monitor engagement, and analyze performance.
- **Popular Tools**: Hootsuite, Buffer, Sprout Social.
- **Key Features**: Content scheduling, social listening, analytics, team collaboration.

Case Study Example:

An e-commerce brand used Hootsuite to automate their social media posting schedule, freeing up 15 hours per week for strategy development, which contributed to a 50% increase in follower growth.

Implementing Automation in Your Sales Funnel

Here's how to implement automation throughout different stages of your sales funnel:

1. Lead Generation

•**Automated Forms**: Use forms on your website to capture leads effortlessly. Integrate these forms with your CRM to ensure leads are auto-logged.

•**Chatbots**: Deploy chatbots on your site to engage visitors and capture lead information.

Example: A B2B company implemented chatbots on their landing pages, increasing lead capture by 40% through immediate and interactive engagement.

2. Lead Nurturing

•**Drip Campaigns**: Set up email sequences to nurture leads over time. Each email should provide value and move the prospect closer to a purchase decision.

•**Content Delivery**: Automate the delivery of content based on lead behavior. If a lead downloads a guide, follow up with relevant articles or case studies.

Example: An online education platform used drip campaigns to nurture course registrants, resulting in a 35% increase in course completion rates.

3. Sales Engagement

•**Task Automation**: Automate tasks like follow-up reminders and appointment scheduling to ensure timely engagement without manual effort.

•**Personalized Outreach**: Use CRM data to automate personalized email and phone outreach based on lead behavior and interests.

Example: A SaaS company integrated task automation in their CRM to ensure no follow-up was missed, reducing lead response time by 50% and increasing sales by 15%.

4. Closing the Sale

•**Proposal Automation**: Automate the creation and sending of sales proposals, ensuring they are customized and timely.

•**E-Signatures**: Use e-signature tools to streamline contract signing and reduce the friction in the closing process.

Example: A consulting firm used e-signature tools to expedite contract signing, cutting down the closing cycle by 30%.

5. Post-Sale Engagement

•**Onboarding Sequences**: Automate welcome and onboarding email sequences to ensure new customers start off on the right foot.

•**Feedback and Reviews**: Automate requests for feedback and reviews post-purchase to build social proof and address any issues proactively.

Example: An online retailer automated post-purchase follow-ups asking for reviews, resulting in a 25% increase in positive customer reviews on their website.

Scaling with Automation

Scaling your business means handling a growing number of leads, customers, and interactions efficiently. Here's how automation helps:

- ***Consistency:*** Automation ensures that every lead receives the same level of attention and engagement, reducing the risk of human error and maintaining brand consistency.

- ***Data-Driven Decisions:*** Automation tools provide valuable insights and analytics, allowing you to make data-driven decisions to optimize your sales strategy.

- ***Increased Productivity:*** By automating repetitive tasks, your team can focus on high-impact activities such as strategy development, creative work, and personal engagement.

- ***Personalization at Scale:*** Automation allows you to deliver personalized experiences to a large audience without manual effort, building stronger relationships and driving loyalty.

Action Steps for Implementing Automation:

---

1. **Select the Right Tools**: Choose automation tools that align with your business needs and integrate seamlessly with your existing systems.

2. **Map Your Sales Funnel**: Identify stages in your sales funnel where automation can add the most value and implement

changes incrementally.

3. **Customize and Personalize**: Ensure your automated messages and workflows are personalized based on customer data and behavior.

4. **Monitor and Optimize**: Continuously monitor the performance of your automation efforts and make adjustments based on data insights.

Automation and technology are *powerful allies* in scaling your sales efforts efficiently. By implementing the right tools and strategies, you can streamline processes, nurture leads effectively, and focus your energy on activities that drive the most value. Once you embrace these tools, you can watch your efficiency—and sales—skyrocket!

12

Analyzing & Improving Strategies

Measuring What Matters

Hey, strategy analyst! In the world of sales, what gets measured, gets improved. Analyzing your sales and marketing efforts allows you to *understand* what's working, what's not, and where to focus your resources for **maximum impact**.

In this chapter, we'll delve into the importance of analytics, the key metrics to monitor, and how to use data insights to refine and improve your strategies. Ready to turn data into actionable insights and drive continuous improvement?

The Importance of Analytics

Analytics is the backbone of informed decision-making. Here's why it's crucial:

1. **Identifying Strengths and Weaknesses**: Analytics help

you pinpoint areas where your strategies are excelling and where they need improvement.

2. **Optimizing Resources**: By understanding the effectiveness of different tactics, you can allocate resources more efficiently.

3. **Driving Continuous Improvement**: Regular analysis enables you to make iterative improvements, keeping your strategies aligned with changing market dynamics.

4. **Enhancing Customer Understanding**: Data insights offer a deeper understanding of customer behavior, preferences, and pain points, allowing for more personalized engagement.

Key Metrics to Monitor

Monitoring the right metrics is essential for gaining meaningful insights. Here are some key metrics across different stages of the sales funnel:

Lead Generation Metrics

- **Website Traffic**: Track the number of visitors to your website, their source, and behavior.
- **Lead Conversion Rate**: Measure the percentage of website visitors who convert into leads (e.g., by filling out a form).

- **Cost Per Lead (CPL)**: Calculate the cost of acquiring a lead through different channels.

Lead Nurturing Metrics

- **Email Open Rates**: Monitor the percentage of recipients who open your emails.
- **Click-Through Rates (CTR)**: Track the percentage of email recipients who click on links within your emails.
- **Engagement Rates**: Measure interactions with your content, such as likes, shares, and comments on social media.

Sales Engagement Metrics

- **Response Time**: Measure the average time it takes to respond to leads.
- **Follow-Up Rate**: Track the consistency of follow-up communications with leads.
- **Meeting and Call Cadence**: Monitor the frequency and effectiveness of meetings or calls with potential customers.

Closing Metrics

- **Win Rate**: Calculate the percentage of deals closed successfully out of the total opportunities.
- **Sales Cycle Length**: Measure the average time it takes to close a deal from initial contact to final sale.
- **Average Deal Size**: Track the average revenue generated per closed deal.

Post-Sale Metrics

- **Customer Satisfaction (CSAT)**: Use surveys to measure customer satisfaction levels.
- **Net Promoter Score (NPS)**: Calculate the likelihood of customers recommending your product or service.
- **Churn Rate**: Measure the percentage of customers who stop using your product or service over a specific period.

Tools for Analytics

Leverage analytics tools to track, measure, and analyze your performance effectively. Here are some popular options:

1. Google Analytics

Ideal for tracking website traffic, user behavior, and conversion rates:

•**Features**: Real-time data, audience insights, behavior flow, conversion tracking, custom reports.

•**Use Case**: Monitor which web pages drive the most traffic and conversions, and understand user navigation patterns.

2. CRM Systems

Track and analyze sales performance, customer interactions, and pipeline progress:

•**Features**: Sales pipeline management, lead tracking, task automation, analytics dashboards.

•**Top Tools**: Salesforce, HubSpot, Zoho CRM.

•**Use Case**: Analyze your sales pipeline to identify bottlenecks and improve deal conversion rates.

3. Email Marketing Platforms

Measure the effectiveness of your email campaigns:

•**Features**: Open rates, click-through rates, bounce rates, segmentation, A/B testing.

•**Top Tools**: Mailchimp, ActiveCampaign, ConvertKit.

•**Use Case**: Test different email subject lines and content to determine what drives higher engagement.

4. Social Media Analytics Tools

Track social media performance and engagement:

- **Features**: Engagement metrics, follower growth, content performance, social listening.
- **Top Tools**: Hootsuite, Buffer, Sprout Social.
- **Use Case**: Identify which social media posts resonate most with your audience and optimize your content strategy accordingly.

Using Data Insights for Improvement

Analytics provide *valuable* insights, but it's the **action** you take based on these insights that drives improvement. Here's how to use data to refine your strategies:

1. Set Clear Goals and Benchmarks

Establish clear goals and benchmarks for your metrics. This allows you to measure progress accurately and identify areas that need attention.

- **Example**: Set a goal to increase your lead conversion rate by 10% over the next quarter, and define the specific steps to achieve this.

2. Identify Patterns and Trends

Look for patterns and trends in your data to understand what's driving performance.

- **Example**: If you notice a high engagement rate for video content, consider incorporating more videos into your content strategy.

3. Conduct A/B Testing

Use A/B testing to compare different variables and determine what works best.

•**Example**: Test different email subject lines to see which one generates higher open rates or test different call-to-action phrases to see which drives more conversions.

4. Iterate and Optimize

Continuously iterate on your strategies based on data insights. Make incremental adjustments and measure the impact.

•**Example**: If you find that a certain sales technique is working well, refine and deploy it more broadly. Conversely, if something isn't working, adjust or eliminate it.

5. Solicit Feedback

Regularly solicit feedback from your team and customers to complement your data insights.

•**Example**: Conduct team meetings to discuss performance metrics and gather ideas for improvement. Use customer surveys to get direct feedback on their experience.

> **Action Steps for Analyzing and Improving Strategies:**

1. **Choose the Right Metrics**: Identify and track key performance metrics across different stages of the sales funnel.

2. **Leverage Analytics Tools**: Use tools like Google Analytics, CRM systems, email marketing platforms, and social media analytics.

3. **Set Goals and Benchmarks**: Establish clear goals and benchmarks to measure progress and success.

4. **Identify Patterns and Trends**: Analyze data to uncover patterns and trends that drive performance.

5. **Conduct A/B Testing**: Use A/B testing to optimize different variables in your strategies.

6. **Iterate and Optimize**: Continuously refine your strategies based on data insights and feedback.

Data-driven decision-making is the *key* to continuous improvement and sustained success. By diligently analyzing your performance, setting clear goals, and applying actionable insights, you'll refine your strategies and drive better outcomes.

Part V

Real-World Applications & Case Studies

13

Success Stories

Learning from the Real World

You're becoming quite the success seeker! One of the most powerful ways to understand and implement sales strategies is by learning from real-world examples. Success stories and case studies provide invaluable insights into how these strategies have been applied and the results they've achieved.

In this chapter, we'll explore detailed case studies of businesses that have successfully utilized online sales techniques, social media marketing, and email campaigns to *drive growth*. By examining their journeys, you'll gain practical knowledge and inspiration to apply these strategies to your own business.

Case Study 1: E-Commerce Breakthrough with Email Marketing

Business Overview: A small e-commerce store specializing in eco-friendly home goods faced challenges in increasing their customer base and sales. They decided to leverage email marketing to nurture leads and drive conversions.

Strategy and Execution:

1. **Building the Email List:**

◦Implemented opt-in forms on the website offering a 10% discount for new subscribers.
◦Expanded the list through social media promotions and collaborations.

2. **Segmented Email Campaigns:**

◦Segmented the list based on customer behavior and interests (e.g., buyers of reusable kitchen products vs. eco-friendly cleaning supplies).
◦Crafted tailored email content for each segment focusing on product benefits, usage tips, and eco-friendly living.

3. **Automated Drip Campaigns:**

◦Set up a welcome email series that gradually introduced new customers to the brand and product offerings.

◦Used birthday and anniversary emails with special discounts and personalized messages.

4. **A/B Testing:**

  ◦Conducted A/B testing on email subject lines and call-to-action buttons to optimize open and click-through rates.

Results and Impact:

- **List Growth**: Increased email list by 200% within six months.

- **Engagement**: Achieved a 45% open rate and a 20% click-through rate on segmented emails.

- **Sales Increase**: Saw a 35% increase in sales attributed to email marketing campaigns.

- **Customer Loyalty**: Built stronger relationships with customers, leading to repeat purchases and referrals.

- **Takeaway:** Personalized, segmented email campaigns with valuable content and strategic automation can significantly boost engagement and sales in e-commerce.

Case Study 2: Social Media Mastery for a Fitness Brand

Business Overview: A fitness brand offering online workout programs and nutritional supplements aimed to expand its reach and increase subscriptions. They focused on leveraging Instagram and Facebook to connect with their target audience.

Strategy and Execution:

1. **Content Creation:**

    ◦ Developed a mix of instructional workout videos, nutritional tips, customer testimonials, and behind-the-scenes content.

    ◦ Maintained a consistent posting schedule with high-quality visuals and engaging captions.

2. **Community Engagement:**

    ◦ Created a fitness challenge with a branded hashtag (#FitWithUsChallenge) encouraging followers to share their progress and experiences.

    ◦ Engaged with followers by responding to comments, messages, and featuring user-generated content.

3. **Influencer Partnerships:**

    ◦ Collaborated with fitness influencers to promote the brand and its programs.

DIGITAL DEALMAKERS

○ Offered influencers exclusive discount codes to share with their followers.

4. Targeted Ads:

○ Ran targeted Facebook and Instagram ads to reach specific demographics interested in fitness and wellness.
○ Used video ads showcasing real transformations and success stories.

Results and Impact:

- **Follower Growth**: Grew Instagram followers from 10,000 to 50,000 in eight months.

- **Engagement**: Increased engagement rates through consistent content and interactive challenges.

- **Conversions**: Achieved a 40% increase in online program subscriptions and a 30% increase in nutritional supplement sales.

- **Brand Awareness**: Enhanced brand visibility and credibility through influencer partnerships.

- **Takeaway:** Consistent, high-quality content and active community engagement, combined with strategic influencer partnerships and targeted advertising, can significantly boost social media presence and drive sales.

Case Study 3: Automation in a B2B SaaS Company

Business Overview: A B2B SaaS company offering marketing automation software aimed to scale their sales efforts and improve lead conversion rates. They implemented CRM and marketing automation tools to streamline processes and improve efficiency.

Strategy and Execution:

1. **Lead Capture and Segmentation:**

   ◦ Utilized lead capture forms on the website with gated content (e.g., eBooks, whitepapers) to gather leads.
   ◦ Segmented leads based on company size, industry, and interaction history.

2. **Automated Lead Nurturing:**

   ◦Developed automated email drip campaigns to nurture leads over time.
   ◦Personalized emails based on lead behavior, such as email opens, link clicks, and webinar participation.

3. **Sales Task Automation:**

　○Automated follow-up reminders, call scheduling, and task assignments within the CRM.

　○Implemented proposal automation tools for seamless document creation and e-signatures.

4. **Performance Tracking:**

　○Used analytics tools to monitor lead engagement, sales pipeline progress, and conversion rates.

　○Conducted regular A/B testing on email content and workflows to optimize performance.

Results and Impact:

- **Lead Conversion**: Improved lead conversion rate by 25% through personalized lead nurturing and timely follow-ups.

- **Sales Productivity**: Increased sales team productivity by 30% due to automated task management and proposal creation.

- **Customer Onboarding**: Enhanced the customer onboarding experience with automated welcome sequences and product tutorials, resulting in higher retention rates.

- **Revenue Growth**: Saw a 20% increase in annual recurring revenue attributable to the combined automation efforts.

Takeaway: Leveraging CRM and marketing automation tools can streamline sales processes, enhance lead nurturing, and significantly boost conversion rates in a B2B environment.

Action Steps for Applying Learnings:

1. **Identify Your Goals**: Clearly define what you want to achieve—be it list growth, follower engagement, lead conversion, or revenue increase.

2. **Choose the Right Tools**: Select tools that align with your business needs and integrate seamlessly with your existing systems.

3. **Personalize Communication**: Tailor your content and messages to the specific needs and behaviors of your audience.

4. **Leverage Data**: Use analytics to track performance, conduct A/B testing, and make data-driven decisions.

5. **Engage Actively**: Maintain consistent engagement with your audience through personalized interactions, community building, and responding to feedback.

Success stories and case studies provide valuable insights into how different businesses have effectively implemented sales and marketing strategies. By learning from their experiences and applying the best practices to your own efforts, you can drive *significant* growth and achieve **remarkable** results. Let's apply these strategies and watch your business thrive!

14

Common Mistakes and How to Avoid Them

Learning from Pitfalls

Even the best sales strategies can falter if plagued by common mistakes. Recognizing and avoiding these pitfalls is *crucial* for maintaining momentum and achieving **sustained success**.

In this chapter, we'll delve into some of the most frequent mistakes made in online sales, along with actionable advice on how to avoid them. Let's navigate these potential hazards and keep your sales efforts on track!

Mistake 1: Ignoring Your Audience's Needs

The Problem: Many businesses fall into the trap of focusing more on their products and services than on the needs and pain points of their audience. This often results in misaligned messaging and lost sales opportunities.

How to Avoid It:

1. **Customer-Centric Approach:** Place your audience's needs at the center of your strategy. Use surveys, polls, and interviews to gather insights into their challenges and desires.
2. **Create Detailed Personas:** Develop comprehensive customer personas based on real data. Tailor your messaging and content to address these personas' specific needs.
3. **Continuous Feedback:** Actively seek and analyze feedback from your audience. Use this feedback to refine your products, services, and marketing strategies.

Mistake 2: Overlooking the Importance of Mobile Optimization

The Problem: In an increasingly mobile world, failing to optimize your website and emails for mobile devices can result in a poor user experience and lost sales.

How to Avoid It:

- **Responsive Design:** Ensure your website and emails are designed responsively to adapt to various screen sizes. Use mobile-friendly templates and test across devices.

- **Fast Loading Times:** Optimize images and minimize code to improve loading times on mobile devices. Use tools like Google PageSpeed Insights to identify and fix issues.

- **User-Friendly Navigation:** Simplify navigation for mobile users. Use clear menus, clickable buttons, and intuitive design elements that enhance the mobile experience.

Mistake 3: Neglecting Content Quality

The Problem: High-quality content is essential for engaging and converting your audience, yet many businesses overlook this aspect, resulting in poorly written, irrelevant, or infrequent content.

How to Avoid It:

1. **Strategic Content Plan:** Develop a content strategy that aligns with your goals and addresses your audience's needs. Create a content calendar to ensure consistency.
2. **Invest in Quality:** Focus on creating high-quality content that provides value, whether it's blog posts, videos, infographics, or social media updates. Consider hiring experienced writers or content creators.
3. **SEO Best Practices:** Optimize your content for search engines using relevant keywords, meta descriptions, and quality backlinks to improve visibility and reach.

Mistake 4: Inconsistent Branding

The Problem: Inconsistent branding across different platforms and marketing materials can confuse your audience and weaken your brand identity.

How to Avoid It:

1. **Brand Guidelines:** Develop and adhere to brand guidelines that define your logo, color scheme, typography, tone of voice, and visual style.
2. **Consistent Messaging:** Ensure your messaging and visuals are consistent across all touchpoints—website, social media, emails, and advertising.
3. **Regular Audits:** Conduct regular brand audits to identify and rectify inconsistencies. Involve your team in maintaining and reinforcing brand standards.

Mistake 5: Neglecting Follow-Up

The Problem: Many sales opportunities are lost due to a lack of timely and persistent follow-up. Prospects may forget or lose interest if not engaged consistently.

How to Avoid It:

1. **Automated Follow-Up Systems:** Use CRM and email marketing tools to automate and schedule follow-up emails. Set reminders for manual follow-ups when necessary.

2. **Personalized Communication:** Tailor your follow-up messages to the prospect's specific interests and previous interactions. Show that you remember and value their engagement.

3. **Multi-Touch Approach:** Use multiple touchpoints for follow-up, including emails, phone calls, social media messages, and retargeting ads to maintain engagement.

Mistake 6: Failing to Analyze and Adapt

The Problem: Not analyzing performance data can lead to stagnant strategies and missed improvement opportunities. Relying on assumptions rather than data can steer you in the wrong direction.

How to Avoid It:

1. **Regular Performance Reviews:** Schedule regular reviews of your analytics and performance metrics. Use tools like Google Analytics, CRM reports, and social media analytics.

2. **Actionable Insights:** Focus on deriving actionable insights from your data. Identify trends, strengths, weaknesses, and opportunities for improvement.

3. **Agility and Adaptation:** Be prepared to pivot and adapt your strategies based on data insights. Continuous optimization is key to staying relevant and effective.

Mistake 7: Over-Reliance on Automation

The Problem: While automation is a powerful tool, over-reliance on it can lead to impersonal interactions and a disconnect from your audience.

How to Avoid It:

1. **Balanced Approach:** Use automation for repetitive tasks and efficiency but ensure a human touch in customer interactions where it matters.
2. **Human Oversight:** Regularly review and tweak automated workflows to ensure they remain relevant and personalized. Complement automation with personalized follow-ups and support.
3. **Customer Feedback:** Solicit and act on customer feedback to maintain a balance between automation and personal engagement.

Action Steps for Avoiding Common Mistakes:

---

1. **Know Your Audience**: Regularly gather and analyze customer data to stay in tune with their needs and preferences.

2. **Optimize for Mobile**: Ensure your online presence is fully optimized for mobile devices.

3. **Maintain High Content Quality**: Prioritize creating valuable and engaging content consistently.

4. **Ensure Consistent Branding**: Develop and adhere to comprehensive brand guidelines.

5. **Follow Up Diligently**: Implement automated follow-ups while maintaining a personal touch.

6. **Analyze and Adapt**: Regularly review performance data and make data-driven decisions.

7. **Balance Automation with Human Touch**: Use automation wisely and complement it with personal engagement.

Avoiding common mistakes and learning from them is crucial for maintaining a successful and *sustainable* online sales strategy. By staying vigilant and proactive, you can navigate these pitfalls and set your business on the path to **continuous growth and success**.

15

Creating Your Personalized Sales Blueprint

Designing Your Path to Success

Now that you've absorbed a wealth of knowledge about online sales, it's time to synthesize those insights into a customized plan *tailored* to your unique business. A personalized sales blueprint will serve as your roadmap, guiding you through the steps to achieve your sales goals and grow your business **effectively**.

In this chapter, we'll break down the process of creating this blueprint, covering everything from setting goals to developing actionable strategies and monitoring progress. Ready to craft a clear, strategic sales plan that sets you up for success? Let's dive in!

Step 1: Define Your Sales Goals

Your sales goals set the foundation for your blueprint and provide a clear target to aim for. Goals should be Specific, Measurable, Achievable, Relevant, and Time-bound (SMART).

1. **Specific**: Clearly define what you want to achieve. Avoid vague goals.

    a. **Example**: Increase online sales revenue by 20%.

2. **Measurable**: Ensure your goals can be quantified.

    a. **Example**: Add 500 new email subscribers in the next three months.

3. **Achievable**: Set goals that are challenging but realistic.

    a. ○**Example**: Improve lead conversion rate from 5% to 10%.

4. **Relevant**: Align goals with your overall business objectives.

    a. ○**Example**: Increase the number of repeat customers to enhance customer loyalty.

5. **Time-bound**: Set a deadline for achieving your goals.

    a. ○**Example**: Achieve a 15% increase in social media engagement within six months.

Step 2: Understand Your Audience and Market

A deep understanding of your audience and market dynamics is critical for crafting effective strategies.

1. **Customer Personas**: Revisit your customer personas to ensure your strategies are aligned with their needs and behaviors.

    ◦**Example**: Persona A: Tech-savvy millennials looking for sustainability in products.

2. **Market Research**: Conduct thorough market research to identify trends, opportunities, and competition.

    ◦**Example**: Identify a rising trend of eco-friendly products in your industry.

3. **Competitive Analysis**: Analyze your competitors' strengths and weaknesses to identify gaps and opportunities.

    ◦**Example**: Competitor X excels in customer service but lacks in personalized product recommendations.

Step 3: Develop Your Sales Strategies

Based on your goals and audience insights, develop targeted sales strategies for each stage of your sales funnel.

Lead Generation

- **SEO and Content Marketing**: Create high-quality, SEO-optimized content to attract organic traffic.

    ◦ **Example**: Publish blog posts and whitepapers addressing sustainability in products.

- **Social Media Marketing**: Leverage social media platforms to reach and engage potential customers.

- **Example**: Run Instagram campaigns showcasing eco-friendly product lines.

- **Email List Building**: Use lead magnets and sign-up forms to grow your email list.

  - **Example**: Offer a free guide on sustainable living in exchange for email subscriptions.

Lead Nurturing

- **Drip Email Campaigns**: Create automated email sequences to nurture leads over time.

  - **Example**: Develop an onboarding email series introducing new subscribers to your brand values and products.

- **Personalized Content**: Tailor content to specific segments based on their interests and behaviors.

  - **Example**: Send personalized emails to subscribers interested in eco-friendly kitchen products.

Sales Engagement

- **Customer Relationship Management (CRM)**: Use a CRM system to manage interactions and track progress.

- **Example**: Use HubSpot to segment leads and track engagement.

- **Follow-Up Strategies**: Implement consistent and personalized follow-up strategies.

  - **Example**: Follow up with potential customers who visited your product pages but did not purchase.

Closing the Sale

- **Discounts and Incentives**: Offer limited-time discounts or special offers to encourage purchases.

  - **Example**: Provide a 10% discount for first-time buyers.

- **Social Proof**: Use testimonials and reviews to build credibility and trust.

  - **Example**: Feature customer success stories and positive reviews on product pages.

Post-Sale Engagement

- **Onboarding Programs**: Create onboarding programs to ensure a smooth customer experience.

  - **Example**: Send welcome emails with usage tips and resources.

- **Loyalty Programs**: Develop loyalty programs to encourage repeat purchases.
    - **Example**: Offer points for each purchase that can be redeemed for discounts.

Step 4: Implement Automation and Technology

Leverage automation tools and technology to streamline processes and enhance efficiency.

- **Email Marketing Automation**: Use platforms like Mailchimp or ActiveCampaign for automated campaigns.
    - **Example**: Automate welcome email series and abandoned cart reminders.
- **CRM Systems**: Implement CRM tools like Salesforce or Zoho to manage customer relationships and sales pipelines.
    - **Example**: Track lead interactions and automate follow-up reminders.
- **Analytics Tools**: Use analytics to monitor performance and make data-driven decisions.
    - **Example**: Use Google Analytics to track website traffic and conversion rates.

Step 5: Monitor and Optimize

Regularly review your progress and make adjustments based on data insights.

- **Performance Metrics**: Monitor key performance metrics to track progress towards your goals.

  - **Example**: Weekly review of conversion rates and engagement metrics.

- **Regular Reviews**: Schedule regular strategy reviews to assess performance and identify areas for improvement.

  - **Example**: Monthly team meetings to discuss progress and brainstorm optimizations.

- **A/B Testing**: Conduct A/B testing to refine and optimize your strategies.

  - **Example**: Test different email subject lines to see which generates higher open rates.

Action Steps for Creating Your Sales Blueprint:

- **Define SMART Goals**: Establish specific, measurable, achievable, relevant, and time-bound goals.

- **Understand Your Audience**: Conduct thorough research to align strategies with audience needs and market trends.

- **Develop Targeted Strategies**: Create tailored sales strategies for each stage of the sales funnel.

- **Leverage Automation**: Use automation tools and technology to streamline and enhance your processes.

- **Monitor and Optimize**: Regularly review performance metrics and adjust strategies based on data insights.

Creating a personalized sales blueprint is about aligning your goals, understanding your audience, developing targeted strategies, leveraging technology, and continuously optimizing based on performance data. By following these steps, you'll have a clear and actionable roadmap to guide your sales efforts and drive remarkable results.

Part VI

Conclusion & Bonus Chapters

16

Conclusion

The Journey of Mastery

Congratulations, sales trailblazer! You've journeyed through the depths of online sales techniques, from understanding your market to mastering the close and leveraging cutting-edge technology. This book has equipped you with a wealth of strategies, insights, and actionable steps to elevate your sales game and achieve remarkable success.

As we wrap up, let's reflect on what you've learned, encourage you to stay the course, and provide some final thoughts on continuous growth and success.

Recap of Key Techniques

Throughout this book, you've explored a variety of powerful techniques designed to help you excel in online sales. Here's a quick recap:

1. **Understanding Your Market**: Identifying and targeting

your ideal audience through detailed market research and customer personas.

2. **Building an Irresistible Online Presence**: Creating a compelling, consistent brand across social media platforms and digital channels.

3. **Crafting Your Value Proposition**: Developing a unique, clear, and compelling value proposition that differentiates you from competitors.

4. **Content is King**: Producing high-quality, engaging content to attract, educate, and convert your audience.

5. **Social Media Marketing Techniques**: Leveraging platform-specific strategies to engage and grow your social media following.

6. **Email Marketing – The Silent Closer**: Utilizing personalized, segmented email campaigns to nurture leads and drive conversions.

7. **The Psychology of Selling**: Understanding buyer behavior and leveraging psychological principles to influence purchasing decisions.

8. **Mastering the Close**: Employing effective closing techniques in video interactions, phone calls, in-person meetings, and live social media sessions.

9. **Turning Leads into Loyal Customers**: Nurturing leads through personalized interactions and creating seamless, memorable customer experiences.

10. **Automation and Technology**: Streamlining processes with CRM systems, marketing automation, and analytics to drive efficiency and scalability.

11. **Analyzing and Improving Strategies**: Using data insights to continuously optimize and refine your sales strategies.

12. **Success Stories**: Learning from real-world applications and case studies to inspire and guide your efforts.

13. **Avoiding Common Mistakes**: Identifying and steering clear of common pitfalls to ensure sustained success.

14. **Creating Your Personalized Sales Blueprint**: Crafting a tailored sales plan to guide your efforts and achieve your goals.

Encouragement and Motivation

The world of online sales is dynamic and constantly evolving. Success requires persistence, adaptability, and a commitment to learning and growth. Here are some final words of encouragement:

- **Embrace the Journey**: Success in sales doesn't happen overnight. Embrace the journey, celebrate small victories, and learn from every setback.

- **Stay Curious**: Keep your curiosity alive. Stay updated with the latest trends, technologies, and best practices in online sales.

- **Be Resilient**: Challenges and rejections are part of the process. Stay resilient, learn from every experience, and keep moving forward.

- **Build Relationships**: Focus on building genuine relationships with your customers. Personal connections foster loyalty and drive long-term success.

- **Adapt and Innovate**: The digital landscape is ever-changing. Be willing to adapt and innovate to stay ahead of the competition.

Final Thoughts and Next Steps

As you embark on the next phase of your journey, remember that the true power of sales lies in providing value, building trust, and creating memorable experiences for your customers. Your dedication to mastering these techniques and continuously improving will pave the way for sustained success.

Here are the next steps to keep you on track:

1. **Implement What You've Learned**: Start applying the strategies and techniques from this book to your daily sales efforts. Take action and monitor your progress.

2. **Seek Feedback**: Regularly seek feedback from customers, peers, and mentors. Use this feedback to refine your approach and improve continuously.

3. **Stay Connected**: Join communities, attend webinars, and connect with industry peers to stay informed and inspired.

4. **Set New Goals**: As you achieve your current goals, set new, ambitious goals to continue pushing yourself and your business forward.

5. **Celebrate Successes**: Take time to celebrate your successes and acknowledge the hard work and dedication that got you there.

You're now equipped with the knowledge, strategies, and tools to excel in online sales and create a thriving business. The journey ahead is filled with opportunities and challenges, but with your *passion, resilience, and commitment to excellence,* you can achieve remarkable success.

Thank you for taking this journey with me. Here's to your continued growth, success, and the *countless* sales victories that lie ahead. Go out there, make your mark, and show the world the power of digital dealmakers!

17

Ready to Dive Deeper?

NEXT STEPS

You *love* these strategies but you're a little overwhelmed or confused on how to actually get this all done and implement it into your business. You want someone to hold your hand and show you click by click what to do? Or maybe you're struggling with seeing the sales from your current business?

Sound's like your ready for my step-by-step training to show you exactly how to accomplish what we've discussed in here and I've got exclusive access to 14 days of done-for-you email campaigns and special *added* bonuses to give you the leg up in turning your business into a *money* machine.

In the Legacy Builders Program, you're not just getting the full education within the course on how to make $300-$900 per day closing sales online—you're joining a community dedicated to supporting your growth and success and given a done-for-you master resell rights product to get you started.

Your business is completely automated for you, you never need to deal with inventory or customer service. You are handed **all** the tools and marketing training you need to become a self-made millionaire completely online. This is unlike any other "*course*" I have taken, this comes with a full mentorship, which people would typically pay thousands a month for, but its all included with your one time purchase! The only way you are not successful with this proven blueprint is if you don't try. This will change your life, just as it has mine.

Taking the leap, investing in yourself and believing in yourself is the key to unlock your full potential of growth online and to take your business to the next level.

By the end of the training you will have a fully function website with sales funnels, a solid foundation of how to create content that converts, how to drive traffic, and how to create digital products to sell online for passive income. *With the payment plan option you get access to the complete course for $0 this month and pay only $46 starting your second month.*

For a limited time, get exclusive bonuses with your purchase of the Legacy Builder's Program only when you purchase here...all for just the price of the course!

Exclusive Bonus Materials:

- **6 extra MRR products** to propel your sales immediately (valued at over $300)

1. **How to Achieve Financial Freedom** e-book w/MRR/PLR ($47)

2. **The Ultimate Social Media Master Planner** with MRR/PLR ($97)

3. **Reel Mastery** with MRR/PLR: How to Create Converting Reels ($47)

4. **The Ultimate Faceless Digital Marketing Playbook** with MRR/PLR: Learn how to build a successful faceless business brand ($97 value)

5. **Stop The Scroll** with MRR/PLR: Utilize insider strategies, tricks and tips that get your viewer to stop scrolling and watch your content ($17)

6. **30 Story Slides Templates** with MRR/PLR: Already done-for-you sales converting story slides ($37 value)

[Purchase Access to the Legacy Builder's Program Here]

www.marissarosemedia.com/dailypaybusiness

Available Add-On's

- **High Impact Inbox:** 14 Day Email Campaign for high converting leads $27

- 300 Chat GPT Prompts to leverage AI 100 Hooks, 100 CTA's, 90 Day of Content Ideas in my **Social Media Blueprint** $27

18

Bonus Chapter Part 1

Staying Ahead in Online Sales

Future-Proofing Your Sales Strategy

I knew you were craving more for your business! Let's dive into some future thoughts. The landscape of online sales is continually evolving, and *staying ahead* requires agility, continuous learning, and a forward-thinking mindset. In this bonus chapter, we'll explore the trends, technologies, and best practices that will keep you at the forefront of the industry.

Embracing Emerging Technologies

Technology is a driving force behind the evolution of online sales. Here are some emerging technologies you should keep an eye on:

1. Artificial Intelligence (AI) and Machine Learning

AI and machine learning can revolutionize your sales processes by providing deeper insights, automating tasks, and personalizing customer interactions.

•**Chatbots**: Use AI-driven chatbots to provide instant customer support and engage website visitors.

•**Predictive Analytics**: Leverage machine learning to predict customer behavior and tailor your marketing strategies accordingly.

•**Personalization Engines**: Employ AI to deliver personalized recommendations and content based on customer preferences and behavior.

Example: An online retailer uses AI to analyze customer purchase history and browsing behavior, providing personalized product recommendations that increase conversion rates.

2. Augmented Reality (AR) and Virtual Reality (VR)

AR and VR can enhance the online shopping experience by allowing customers to visualize products in a more immersive way.

•**AR Product Visualization**: Enable customers to see how products will look in their environment (e.g., furniture in their living room).

•**VR Showrooms**: Create virtual showrooms where customers can explore your products in a simulated environment.

Example: A home decor company offers an AR app that allows customers to visualize how furniture will look in their homes before making a purchase.

3. Voice Search and Smart Assistants

The rise of voice search and smart assistants like Alexa and Google Assistant is changing how consumers search for products and interact with brands.

•**Voice Search Optimization**: Optimize your website content for voice search queries to capture this growing segment.

•**Voice-Activated Shopping**: Develop voice-activated shopping experiences to streamline the purchase process.

Example: An e-commerce brand optimizes its product listings for voice search, resulting in increased traffic from voice-activated devices.

Adapting to Consumer Behavior Shifts

Understanding and adapting to changing consumer behavior is crucial for staying relevant. Here are some key trends to watch:

1. Mobile Commerce

With the increasing use of smartphones, mobile commerce continues to grow. Ensure your online presence is mobile-friendly and provides a seamless experience.

•**Mobile-First Design**: Design your website and email campaigns with a mobile-first approach.

•**Mobile Payments**: Offer convenient mobile payment options like Apple Pay and Google Wallet.

2. Ethical and Sustainable Practices

Consumers are increasingly conscious of the ethical and environmental impact of their purchases. Brands that demonstrate commitment to sustainability and ethical practices can win customer loyalty.

•**Sustainable Products**: Offer eco-friendly products and highlight their benefits.

•**Transparent Practices**: Be transparent about your sourcing, production processes, and environmental impact.

Example: A fashion brand highlights its commitment to sustainability by showcasing eco-friendly materials and ethical production practices, resonating with environmentally conscious consumers.

3. Social Commerce

Social media platforms are evolving into powerful sales channels. Leverage social commerce features to reach and engage your audience directly.

•**Shoppable Posts**: Use shoppable posts on Instagram and Facebook to allow users to purchase products directly from your social media updates.

•**Live Streaming Sales**: Host live streaming events where you showcase products, interact with viewers, and offer exclusive deals.

Example: A beauty brand hosts live streaming events on Instagram where they demonstrate product usage and offer exclusive discounts, driving real-time sales.

Fostering Continuous Learning

To stay ahead, committing to continuous learning and improvement is essential. Here's how to foster a culture of learning:

1. Stay Informed

Regularly consume industry news, articles, podcasts, and webinars to stay updated on the latest trends and best practices.

•**Industry Blogs**: Follow leading industry blogs and thought leaders.

•**Webinars and Conferences**: Attend webinars and virtual conferences to gain insights and network with peers.

2. Invest in Training

Continuously invest in training and development for yourself and your team.

•**Online Courses**: Enroll in online courses to enhance your skills and knowledge.

•**Workshops and Seminars**: Participate in workshops and seminars to learn from experts and practitioners.

3. Encourage Experimentation

Foster a culture of experimentation where new ideas are tested and iterated upon.

•**Pilot Programs**: Launch pilot programs to test new strategies and technologies before full-scale implementation.

- **Feedback Loops**: Create feedback loops to gather insights and refine your approach based on real-world results.

Maintaining Agility and Adaptability

Staying ahead requires the ability to adapt quickly to changing conditions. Here's how to maintain agility:

1. Agile Methodology

Adopt agile methodologies to manage projects and campaigns more effectively.

- **Sprint Planning**: Break projects into smaller sprints with clear goals and deliverables.
- **Iterative Development**: Continuously iterate and adjust based on feedback and performance data.

2. Responsive Strategy

Be prepared to pivot and adjust your strategies based on changing market dynamics and consumer behavior.

- **Real-Time Analytics**: Use real-time analytics to monitor performance and make data-driven decisions.
- **Flexible Planning**: Develop flexible plans that allow for quick adjustments and course corrections.

> **Action Steps for Staying Ahead:**
>
> 1. **Embrace Emerging Technologies**: Explore and implement AI, AR/VR, and voice search to enhance your sales strategy.
>
> 2. **Adapt to Consumer Behavior Shifts**: Align your strategies with trends in mobile commerce, ethical purchasing, and social commerce.
>
> 3. **Foster Continuous Learning**: Stay informed, invest in training, and encourage experimentation within your team.
>
> 4. **Maintain Agility and Adaptability**: Adopt agile methodologies and ensure your strategies are responsive to market changes.

Staying ahead in online sales requires continuous learning, leveraging emerging technologies, adapting to consumer behavior shifts, and maintaining agility. By embracing these principles, you'll not only keep pace with the evolving digital landscape but also position your business for sustained success and growth. Embrace innovation, adapt to change, and drive your business forward into the future!

19

Bonus Chapter Part 2

STAYING MOTIVATED AND ENGAGED

The Drive to Success

While strategy and technique are critical, maintaining long-term motivation and engagement is equally essential for sustained success in online sales. This chapter is dedicated to keeping your *passion alive*, your energy high, and your commitment **unwavering**.

Let's explore practical tips and strategies to help you stay motivated, engaged, and continuously inspired on your journey to becoming a digital sales powerhouse.

Setting Meaningful Goals

Goals give you direction and purpose. Setting meaningful, achievable goals keeps you motivated and engaged.

1. **Short-Term and Long-Term Goals**: Set a mix of short-term and long-term goals to keep yourself motivated and provide a clear path for your efforts.
   - **Example**: Short-term goal: Increase email list by 200 subscribers in one month. Long-term goal: Double annual revenue in the next year.

2. **Personal and Professional Goals**: Balance your professional goals with personal aspirations to maintain overall well-being and satisfaction.
   - **Example**: Professional goal: Develop a new product line. Personal goal: Achieve a work-life balance that allows for personal hobbies and time with family.

3. **Review and Adjust**: Regularly review your goals and adjust them as needed. Celebrate your achievements and set new challenges to keep progressing.
   - **Example**: Conduct quarterly reviews to assess goal progress and make necessary adjustments.

Cultivating a Growth Mindset

A growth mindset encourages continuous learning and resilience in the face of challenges.

1. **Embrace Challenges**: View challenges as opportunities to learn and grow rather than obstacles.

○ **Example**: See a dip in sales as a chance to analyze and improve your strategy rather than a setback.

2. **Learn from Feedback**: Constructive feedback is invaluable for growth. Seek and welcome feedback from customers, peers, and mentors.
○ **Example**: Use customer reviews to identify areas for improvement and refine your products or services.

3. **Celebrate Effort**: Recognize and celebrate the effort put into your work, not just the outcomes.
○ **Example**: Acknowledge the hard work your team puts into launching a new campaign, regardless of immediate results.

Building a Supportive Network

Surrounding yourself with a supportive network of peers, mentors, and like-minded individuals can provide motivation, inspiration, and practical advice.

1. **Join Professional Communities**: Engage with online forums, social media groups, and professional organizations related to your industry.
○ **Example**: Participate in LinkedIn groups focused on digital marketing and sales.

2. **Attend Events and Workshops**: Take part in industry conferences, webinars, and workshops to network and learn from experts.

○**Example**: Attend an annual digital marketing summit to stay updated on the latest trends and technologies.

3. **Find a Mentor**: Seek out a mentor who can offer guidance, support, and perspective based on their experience.
○**Example**: Connect with a seasoned sales professional who can provide monthly guidance and feedback on your progress.

Maintaining Work-Life Balance

A balanced lifestyle is essential for sustained motivation and productivity.

1. **Set Boundaries**: Define clear boundaries between work and personal life to prevent burnout.
○**Example**: Set a specific time to end your workday and commit to it.

2. **Take Breaks**: Regular breaks can rejuvenate your mind and improve focus and creativity.
○**Example**: Follow the Pomodoro Technique—work for 25 minutes, then take a 5-minute break.

3. **Prioritize Self-Care**: Engage in activities that promote physical, mental, and emotional well-being.
○**Example**: Exercise regularly, practice mindfulness, and spend time with loved ones.

Staying Inspired

Inspiration keeps your creativity flowing and your passion alive.

1. **Continuous Learning**: Dedicate time to learning new skills, exploring new ideas, and expanding your knowledge.
   - **Example**: Enroll in an online course on emerging sales technologies.

2. **Creative Outlets**: Engage in creative activities that stimulate your mind and provide a break from routine tasks.
   - **Example**: Experiment with new content formats, like creating videos or starting a podcast.

3. **Successful Role Models**: Follow the journeys of successful individuals and companies to draw inspiration and motivation.
   - **Example**: Read biographies of renowned entrepreneurs or listen to podcasts featuring industry leaders.

Reflecting on Progress

Regular reflection helps you stay connected to your goals and recognize your achievements.

1. **Journaling**: Keep a journal to document your experiences, challenges, successes, and lessons learned.

◦**Example**: Spend 10 minutes each evening reflecting on the day's achievements and areas for improvement.

2. **Celebrating Milestones**: Celebrate both big and small milestones to acknowledge progress and maintain enthusiasm.

◦**Example**: Reward yourself and your team for hitting quarterly targets or successfully launching a new campaign.

3. **Periodic Reviews**: Conduct regular reviews to assess progress, identify areas for growth, and set new goals.

◦**Example**: Schedule monthly or quarterly review meetings with your team to evaluate performance and adjust strategies.

Action Steps for Staying Motivated and Engaged:

---

1. **Set Meaningful Goals**: Define clear, achievable goals that inspire you and provide direction.

2. **Cultivate a Growth Mindset**: Embrace challenges, seek feedback, and celebrate effort.

3. **Build a Supportive Network**: Engage with professional communities, attend events, and find a mentor.

4. **Maintain Work-Life Balance**: Set boundaries, take breaks, and prioritize self-care.

5. **Stay Inspired**: Commit to continuous learning, explore

creative outlets, and follow successful role models.

6. **Reflect on Progress**: Journal, celebrate milestones, and conduct periodic reviews.

Staying motivated and engaged is a *continuous process* that requires intentional effort and a balanced approach. By setting meaningful goals, embracing a growth mindset, building a supportive network, maintaining work-life balance, staying inspired, and reflecting on your progress, you'll sustain your motivation and achieve lasting success in online sales. May you continue to grow, succeed, and inspire others with your passion and dedication.

20

Glossary of Terms

Understanding key terminology is essential for mastering online sales

•**Bounce Rate**: The percentage of visitors who navigate away from a website after viewing only one page.

•**Conversion Rate**: The percentage of visitors who take a desired action, such as making a purchase or filling out a form.

•**CRM (Customer Relationship Management)**: Software used to manage interactions with current and potential customers.

•**CTR (Click-Through Rate)**: The percentage of people who click on a link, ad, or email compared to the total number of viewers.

•**Drip Campaign**: A series of automated emails sent to leads or customers over time.

•**Engagement Rate**: A metric that measures the level of engagement a piece of content receives, typically through likes, comments, shares, and clicks.

•**Lead Magnet**: A valuable resource or incentive offered to prospects in exchange for their contact information.

- **ROI (Return on Investment)**: A measure of the profitability of an investment, calculated as the net profit divided by the cost of the investment.
- **SEO (Search Engine Optimization)**: The practice of optimizing content to improve its ranking on search engines.
- **USP (Unique Selling Proposition)**: The factor that differentiates a product or service from its competitors, often highlighting a unique benefit.

* * *

List of Recommended Tools and Resources

These tools and resources can help you implement the strategies discussed in this book:

Lead Generation

- **Google Analytics**: For tracking website traffic and user behavior.
- **Sumo**: For creating popups and opt-in forms.

Email Marketing

- **Mailchimp**: For email marketing automation and campaign management.
- **ActiveCampaign**: For advanced email marketing and CRM integration.

Social Media Management

- **Hootsuite**: For scheduling and managing social media posts.
- **Buffer**: For planning and publishing social media content.

CRM Systems

- **Salesforce**: For comprehensive customer relationship management.
- **HubSpot**: For CRM, marketing, and sales tools.

Automation and Analytics

- **Zapier**: For connecting and automating workflows between different apps and services.

- **Google Data Studio**: For creating customizable data reports and dashboards.

* * *

Sample Email Templates

Here are some sample email templates to get you started with your email marketing campaigns:

Welcome Email

Subject: Welcome to [Your Brand Name]!

Hi [First Name],

Welcome to the [Your Brand Name] family! We're thrilled to have you on board.

As a thank you for joining us, here's a special gift just for you: [Discount Code/Free Resource].

Stay tuned for more exciting updates, exclusive offers, and valuable content coming your way.

Best wishes,

[Your Name]

[Your Position]

[Your Contact Information]

Abandoned Cart Email

Subject: Did you forget something?

Hi [First Name],

We noticed that you left some amazing items in your cart. Don't worry; your cart is still waiting for you!

[Product Image]

[Product Name]

Complete your purchase now and enjoy [Discount/Free Shipping]!

[Call to Action Button: "Complete My Purchase"]

Best regards,

[Your Name]

[Your Position]

[Your Contact Information]

Post-Purchase Thank You Email

Subject: Thank You for Your Purchase!

Hi [First Name],

Thank you for your purchase! We hope you're excited to receive [Product Name].

Here are some resources to help you get the most out of your new product: [Usage Tips/FAQs/Video Tutorials]

If you have any questions or need assistance, don't hesitate to reach out.

Thank you for choosing [Your Brand Name]!

Sincerely,

[Your Name]

[Your Position]

[Your Contact Information]

* * *

Sample Social Media Posts

Here are some example social media posts to inspire your content:

Instagram Post

Caption: Ready to elevate your style with our new eco-friendly collection?

Tap the link in our bio to shop now and enjoy a special launch discount! #EcoFashion #SustainableLiving

[Image: A visually appealing photo of your new product line]

Facebook Post

Introducing our latest innovation, designed to make your life easier and more sustainable!

Check out our new product line and enjoy an exclusive 20% off your first purchase. Click here to shop: [Link]

#SustainableProducts #Innovation

[Image: Product photo with a call to action]

Twitter Post

Exciting news! Our new collection is live! Shop now and get 10% off your first order. Hurry, offer ends soon! [Link]

#NewArrivals #Shopping #Discount

[Image: Product image]

* * *

Worksheet: Crafting Your Unique Selling Proposition (USP)

Use this worksheet to develop and refine your USP.

1. **Identify Your Unique Features and Benefits**:

° What makes your product or service unique?

° What benefits do you offer that your competitors don't?

2. **Understand Your Target Audience**:

° Who are your ideal customers?

° What are their pain points and needs?

3. **Summarize Your USP**:

° How can you explain your unique value clearly and concisely?

Example Template: "We help [Target Audience] achieve [Desired Outcome] by providing [Unique Feature/Benefit], unlike [Competitor's Offering] which [Competitor's Weakness]."

Checklist: Steps to Building Your Online Sales Funnel

This checklist will guide you through building a comprehensive online sales funnel:

1. **Awareness Stage**:

° Create high-quality content (blogs, videos, infographics).

- Optimize for SEO.
- Promote content on social media.
- Run targeted ads.

2. **Interest Stage**:
- Capture leads with lead magnets and opt-in forms.
- Segment your email list.
- Nurture leads with valuable content and drip campaigns.

3. **Decision Stage**:
- Highlight key benefits and value propositions.
- Offer case studies, testimonials, and social proof.
- Personalize communications.

4. **Action Stage**:
- Provide clear and compelling calls to action.
- Simplify the checkout process.
- Offer incentives like discounts or free shipping.

5. **Retention Stage**:
- Follow up with thank you emails and onboarding guides.
- Implement loyalty programs.
- Regularly engage customers with valuable content and offers.

www.ingramcontent.com/pod-product-compliance
Lightning Source LLC
Chambersburg PA
CBHW071504220526
45472CB00003B/906